# CANCERMAN
## TO
## IRONMAN

Nidhin Valsan is currently serving as Deputy Commissioner of Police in Delhi. This is his first book.

# CANCERMAN TO IRONMAN

A Police Officer's Journey
of Arresting Illness

**NIDHIN VALSAN**

PAN

First published 2024 by Pan
an imprint of Pan Macmillan Publishing India Private Limited
707 Kailash Building
26 K. G. Marg, Delhi 110001
www.panmacmillan.co.in

Pan Macmillan, The Smithson, 6 Briset Street, London EC1M 5NR
Associated companies throughout the world
www.panmacmillan.com

ISBN: 978-81-19300-68-6

Copyright © Nidhin Valsan 2024

The moral rights of the author have been asserted.

All rights reserved. No part of this publication may be reproduced, stored in or introduced into a retrieval system, or transmitted, in any form, or by any means (electronic, mechanical, photocopying, recording or otherwise) without the prior written permission of the publisher.

Any person who does any unauthorized act in relation to this publication may be liable to criminal prosecution and civil claims for damages.

The views expressed in this book are the author's own and the facts reported by him have been verified by the publisher to the extent possible. The publisher hereby disclaims any liability to any party for loss, damages or disruptions caused by the same.

3 5 7 9 8 6 4

This book is sold subject to the condition that it shall not, by way of trade or otherwise, be lent, re-sold, hired out, or otherwise circulated without the publisher's prior consent in any form of binding or cover other than that in which it is published and without a similar condition including this condition being imposed on the subsequent purchaser.

Typeset in Sabon LT Std by SÜRYA, New Delhi
Printed and bound in India by Thomson Press India Ltd.

*For all the cancer fighters and
their family members*

# Foreword

In the pages that follow, readers will embark on a journey as much about the resilience of the human spirit as physical endurance. Nidhin Valsan, an IPS officer, has demonstrated an extraordinary commitment to life and health, not just by surviving a formidable adversary – cancer – but by achieving the near-impossible feat of completing an Ironman triathlon.

Nidhin's battle with non-Hodgkin's lymphoma is proof of the incredible strength and willpower that resides within us all. Diagnosed with this aggressive cancer, he faced the daunting challenge of chemotherapy and the physical and emotional toll that comes with it. Yet his resolve never wavered. His love for his children and his determination to be there for them fuelled his fight against the disease.

After being declared cancer-free, Nidhin didn't just return to a semblance of normalcy; he set his sights on a goal that many would deem unattainable even in peak health. The Ironman triathlon – a gruelling event that includes a 1.9-kilometre swim, a 90-kilometre bike ride and a 21.1-kilometre run – became his new battlefield. Training rigorously, he adopted a lifestyle that prioritized discipline, physical fitness and mental fortitude.

On the day of the event, Nidhin's motivation was not just to finish the race but to send a powerful message to the world. His journey from being a cancer patient to an Ironman is a beacon of hope, proving that with focus and determination, one can overcome the greatest of life's challenges. His story is a poignant reminder that cancer is not a death sentence but a battle that can be fought and won.

Nidhin's account is more than an inspirational tale; it is a call to arms for all those facing similar battles. His experiences underline the importance of a positive mindset, the support of loved ones and the sheer power of the human will. I invite you to delve into and draw inspiration from Nidhin's remarkable journey.

**YUVRAJ SINGH**
Cancer survivor, international cricketer and
Founder, YouWeCan
**July 2024**

# Preface

The most difficult ordeal a person endures is pain without explanation. Pain, physical or mental, is bearable if one understands the underlying cause. It becomes less intense. Sometimes, it's even pleasurable. You might blame yourself or the bad things that have happened in your life. You have a reason and, whether consciously or unconsciously, you like it. The process can be addictive. Though it might leave you depressed.

But if you are experiencing severe pain and do not know why, you are unable to attribute it to anything. Then the pain becomes unbearable. Such was my state from November 2020 to January 2021. I was in excruciating pain, yet no one could explain it. I consulted the best doctors, but none could provide a satisfactory or convincing response. For more than two and a half months, I bore the excruciating pain with no explanation. When I learnt I had cancer, I was more happy than sad. The agony of not knowing had been intolerable. Deep inside I was satisfied, even while my entire world shook around me. At least, I now understood why I was in pain.

In early November 2020 on my way back to my posting in Lakshadweep, after finishing a mid-career training programme (MCTP) at the National Police Academy, Hyderabad, I was required to quarantine – first in Kochi and then in Lakshadweep for twenty days as part of the Lakshadweep administration policy. At the academy, I maintained a fitness regimen, running 5 kilometres every day and 10 kilometres every weekend. However, I began to notice skin irritations across my body. Meanwhile, I received my transfer orders to Goa, a change I welcomed enthusiastically.

While quarantining in Kochi, I stayed in a room with a lovely view from the balcony. Despite my fitness efforts at the academy, I had gained weight due to the delicious local food. So, I took advantage of my time and shed two to three kilograms before moving on to Kavaratti, the capital of Lakshadweep, where I faced another ten-day quarantine. The accommodations were well-equipped with a treadmill, a bench press and a set of dumbbells. One fine day, though, I developed chest pains. I thought, perhaps I had bench-pressed too much.

After completing the quarantine, I rejoined the Lakshadweep administration to finalize my relocation to Goa. On my request, administration gave me fourteen days to move out of the islands to join Goa as per my transfer order. But the chest pain returned. One morning, I woke up to shooting pains – far more intense than what I had experienced in Kochi. From that moment, until my first chemo three months later, there was not a single day without pain – extreme physical pain.

The chest pain gradually became a persistent companion. After the island quarantine, during a meeting, someone cracked a joke and we all started laughing. As soon as I joined in, I felt a stabbing pain on the left side of my chest. Unable to laugh, I clutched at the area, tears streaming down my face. Sachin Sharma IPS, who was sitting next to me, asked with concern, 'Sir, *aap theek toh ho* (are you alright)?'

'It's such a good joke that I started cry-laughing,' I replied.

Intense fatigue soon became a regular feature of my days. At the time I was also winding down a long three-and-half-year tenure at my post and didn't have much work to occupy my mind. I constantly felt the urge to sleep. Yet when I lay down, I couldn't fall asleep, simply lying awake. Any movement, bending down or standing up, felt as though a sharp knife was piercing my lungs and heart.

While I was relocating from the islands, the police and Indian Reserve Battalion (IRBn) staff organized a ceremonial rope-pulling event. It was a proud and emotional moment for everyone, and some of the men even had tears in their eyes. As their commandant, I had always made sure their grievances were heard and addressed. That day, my officers told me that all the Lakshadweep police personnel, IRBn guys and LDCL (Lakshadweep Development Corporation Ltd) staff – I was their MD (Managing Director) for a year and made major changes in the company during my tenure – had displayed my photograph as their WhatsApp statuses. They had laid a red carpet for me at the rope-pulling ceremony, where, right at the beginning, a beautifully decorated open vehicle awaited me. Climbing into the vehicle was painful; my knees and thighs ached, forcing me to bend and hold my knees to manage the ascent. Once atop the jeep, the officers and men pulled the vehicle forward with a large rope tied to the front. As we moved, everyone threw flowers at me. Such a grand send-off was unexpected. I had led them through some tough times – elections, cyclones and the Covid-19 pandemic. When I was leaving, Lakshadweep remained the only green zone in the country, free from Covid-19 infections. Sadly, within a month of my departure, I began to hear about how the virus had started to claim lives, including those of my own men in uniform.

~

It was half past one in the morning in Thalassery, my hometown in Kerala. Alongside me were my wife Remya and our children, Ishaan and Niya, with my parents also under the same roof. What initially seemed like a peaceful night turned into the first of many a restless night to come. I was jolted awake by severe chest pain and a heavy sweat. Both my palms throbbed painfully, as if needles were about to burst through my fingertips, while a sharp knife seemed to tear through my body, slicing my heart open. The rest of the household was sound asleep, and I didn't want to wake them. Though I suspected a heart attack, I knew such events typically involved shoulder and back pain. Instead, I endured severe chest pain and a painfully intense tingling in my fingers and palms. I chose to bear the pain, lying between my five-year-old son and three-year-old daughter. The pain was so overwhelming that I found myself silently screaming, tears streaming down my face. I remained motionless in bed, waiting for the sun to rise yet bracing for what might be my own personal sunset. For the first time, I truly feared I might be dying.

The next morning, a visit to the doctor diagnosed me with cervical spondylosis and emphasized the need to improve my posture. It was also pointed out that I was carrying an undue amount of stress and worry. A large assortment of medications was prescribed to me. My flight to Goa was set from Kochi, to which we were to travel by road from Thalassery. On the way, we stopped at a friend's home for breakfast where, after the meal, I began sorting through my newly acquired medicines. This prompted our host to comment to Remya, 'At such a young age, he is on so many medications!' Indeed, my medicine box was brimming with tablets.

Devoid of rest, fatigue plagued me costantly, and sharp, tingling sensations in my fingers and palms became a regular nuisance. My nights were often interrupted as I found myself waking frequently to use the bathroom.

On reaching Goa with Remya and the kids, we settled into the police officers' mess. The building was so old that at first glance, the rooms seemed to scream for major renovations. However, we had no choice but to wait until the Public Works Department (PWD) assigned us a quarter and allowed us to move there. We ended up staying in the officers' mess for nearly fifty days. Little did I know, these seemingly mundane events were actually the start of a transformative journey within me.

# I
# Diagnosis

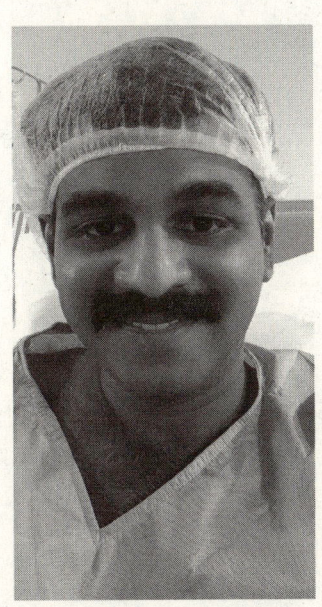

# 1

The chest pain accompanied by sharp, painful sensations in my fingers and palms had become all too familiar. An online search suggested I was suffering from fibromyalgia, a chronic nerve condition marked by persistent tingling and pain in the extremities. With no known cure for fibromyalgia, you typically just have to live with it. The only relief comes from exercises that can help manage the symptoms. The simplest tasks, like buttoning shirts or tearing chapatis and dosas, had become extremely painful due to the pain in my fingers. But at least Google had offered me an explanation.

Soon after arriving in Goa, Remya and I managed to enrol our son Ishaan at a school. Because of the pandemic, the school was only conducting online classes at the time. About a week later, one night around ten o'clock, I woke up again with severe pain in my groin area – similar to the chest pain I'd previously experienced but a hundred times more excruciating. It felt as though my groin was being hacked with a sharp axe. My screams woke up the entire family, including the kids. Trying to soothe them, I said, 'Nothing, baby, *acha* (father) just had a very bad dream; nothing to worry about.' After everyone had calmed down, I went to the bathroom and waited for nearly fifteen minutes for the pain to go away so I could go back to sleep. At 3 a.m., the pain flared up once more, but this time I managed to keep quiet.

'Oh my God, what is happening to me?' I went to the bathroom to look again. Once again the pain subsided after about fifteen minutes, and I tried to go back to sleep. But my mind was racing. 'This doesn't seem like fibromyalgia. These symptoms don't match the ones I had read about. What's this? Why is there pain in my groin? Could this make me sterile? Am I being punished for past sins? No, I've always tried to do right by others. Did I suffer an injury? Or maybe my body's reacting to all the medications? Am I imagining the pain? Do I have a deadly disease? Give me an answer, God!' The thoughts consumed me until I finally fell asleep again.

The pain returned like clockwork at 5 a.m. Following the same grim ritual, I headed to the bathroom and, after some time, the pain subsided. This episode was so severe I thought I had lost control of my bladder. Whatever this was, I decided to see a doctor that very day. Sleep eluded me not just that night but for the next two months.

~

When I awoke, I rushed to Goa Medical College (GMC). In fact, I had arrived so early that I had to wait for the doctors to start their day. I began with an orthopaedic doctor and then moved on to a surgeon for further referrals. Throughout the day, I met with a neurosurgeon, a neurologist and a general physician. It took nearly a week to complete all the tests and get the results. Everyone seemed surprised by the kinds of pain I was experiencing. Initially, the doctors suspected the onset of diabetes, but the results told a different story.

My nerve conduction tests indicated that my nervous system was working at its best. All other blood parameters appeared to be normal as well. However, the magnetic resonance imaging (MRI), a noninvasive medical imaging test, revealed enlarged lymph nodes, which prompted the radiologist to recommend further analyses.

The most confident of all these doctors I consulted was the general physician. His advice still echoes in my mind: 'Sir, you have a stressful job. You're under stress. You don't have any problems. I know many of your colleagues. This type of condition is common among police officers because of the high stress levels.

Nothing to worry about. Go home, practise yoga, keep laughing, drink a few beers, swim in a pool and make love to your wife.' I explained that I had recently arrived in Goa and was not under any stress as I had yet to get my posting orders. He rattled on, 'Sir, from my experience, you don't have anything. It might be some stress from earlier.'

When I asked about the enlarged lymph nodes in my throat, he replied, 'It is very common, sir. Even if you get a mild cold, the lymph nodes will appear. They will vanish after the infection is over. Concentrate on your work. I say again, you don't have anything.'

The neurologist suggested a wait-and-see approach, advising, 'Your nerve conduction test and all parameters appear normal. If you took a lot of medicine in the last few days, your body may have developed an allergy to those medicines.'

During this time, my classmate Dr Anand Warrier, who had studied at All India Institute of Medical Sciences (AIIMS) Delhi and knew me from my days in the Delhi Police, had been closely following my situation. Unlike the others, he took my symptoms seriously and urged me to get a detailed MRI, stating that such severe pain was not typical, even under stress. Unsure of what to do next, I took his advice and he arranged for an appointment with his doctor friend at Manipal Hospital in Goa.

After some time, he called me back and said that the doctor in Goa was out of town, so he had fixed an appointment with another neurologist, recommended by his friend. When I went to her, she examined me thoroughly and said, 'I can't find anything much. Let's stop the medicines for some days and see.' I called Warrier and conveyed the same to him. Still sceptical, he said, 'Let's wait and watch.'

At this point, I was almost convinced that my pain was psychological, stemming from stress. What was causing the stress? I wasn't sure. I didn't have any problems. My certainty reached a full hundred per cent after Dr Benz and Dr Augustus visited me in Goa.

~

Ashish Benz is a close friend and our family doctor. He is a leading gynaecologist in our district and helped deliver our second child. We've been friends since our college days – nearly fifteen years – when he was doing his MBBS at Calicut Medical College, and I was at National Institute of Technology (NIT) Calicut, studying engineering.

He had come to Mumbai for training. Afterwards, he travelled to Mangalore, picked up Augustus and they both drove down to Goa. By this time, I was waiting for my posting orders with the Goa Police and had no work other than attending meetings, so I was free to spend all my time with them.

In the company of doctors, I opened up about all my issues and the ordeal I was facing. I showed them the test results and medical prescriptions I had received in the past three weeks and mentioned what other doctors had told me.

Since senior doctors had already given their opinions, Benz and Augustus agreed with them. Augustus shared a story about a female patient of a friend who was convinced she was pregnant. Despite medical tests indicating otherwise, she truly believed that she was. Can you believe what happened next? Incredibly, her belly started growing as if she were pregnant. Eventually, she had to undergo psychiatric treatment to get back to normal. Augustus believed the mind was very powerful. Whatever it imagined, it could manifest. Especially when one's thoughts obsess over their body.

Indirectly, he was suggesting, 'You are a psycho' – at least, that's how it felt to me. Benz, quoting a famous Malayalam movie dialogue, said, 'You are moving from neurosis to psychosis.' In the film *Manichitrathazhu*, the heroine is a 'psycho' and gradually becomes a complete 'whacko'. A doctor informs her husband about her condition, declaring, 'From neurosis, she is moving towards psychosis.' Implicitly, it seemed everyone believed I was imagining the pain.

By then, I was also convinced. I had spoken with Dr Warrier, who still insisted I undergo a contrast MRI but I dismissed him. 'Bro, it's purely psychological; I know what to do.' But the 'axe chop' pain in my groin was not convinced. While sharing a room with Benz, the pain woke me up one night. I called out to him, and he murmured, 'Don't worry and sleep,' before drifting back to sleep himself.

'I also want that. Just to sleep peacefully,' I wanted to scream at him in frustration. Yet no words came out that night. I tried to sleep but couldn't manage to drift off again.

The next day, he gave me a pain-relieving ointment and stress-relief tablets.

Although I didn't sleep for almost two weeks, I shared some of the most joyful moments with my friends during their visit. We enjoyed a lot, eating good food and exploring the surrounding areas.

∽

Convinced that I was under stress and needed to cool down, I decided to start taking yoga classes. I had never really been a *yoga person*; my body wasn't flexible enough. At the police academy, yoga was part of our physical training, and we had a final test for it. Of all the tests, this one made me the most anxious. I thought yoga was for those who don't want to move much; those afraid of effort, those afraid of pain and gain. Though I didn't believe yoga itself to be harmful, I had never tried it.

I loved running and high-intensity interval training (HIIT), which involves short bursts of intense exercise alternated with recovery periods. On the islands, I used to run at least 5 kilometres and do thirty minutes of HIIT every day. I also loved swimming and led a group of swimmers and completed a swimming expedition as part of a 'Plastic-Free Island' campaign. While working in Bangalore I had learnt karate, and as an ACP in the Delhi Police, I had even tried boxing, stopping only after being badly beaten by an African boxer. I was ready to try anything – except yoga.

To all those proponents of yoga who told me to try it, I would say, 'I am fit enough for running and heavy workouts. I will start doing yoga only after forty. Yoga is for the lazy.'

Five years before I planned to start yoga, at thirty-five, life gave me a whipping for my fitness arrogance. It was like what Rocky Balboa said, 'Life will hit you hard'. Life was hitting me hard now. I was not sleeping; throughout the day I felt tired and sleepy, but I could not sleep, neither during the day nor at night. I just wanted to sleep. When Warrier called me again and asked how I was doing, I told him I just wanted to sleep. I was ready to bear the pain and tolerate fatigue, but I couldn't keep compromising on my sleep. I asked him to give me something to help me sleep. I just wanted to rest – just for one night – and I was ready to do anything for it.

Considering my desperation for sleep, doing yoga seemed like the simplest thing I could do. Running and working out had become increasingly painful, another reason I finally relented to try yoga. My ankles had started hurting, and the right one was swollen. This was surprising, as I hadn't had any accidents or twisted my ankles, yet my right ankle was in too much pain. Even both my knees had developed pain. Bending or folding them had become painful. Before running, I needed to stretch out my legs, which involved twisting my ankles and bending my knees. I noticed that both exercises had started to hurt so much that maybe yoga would be better. At least it might help increase my flexibility – maybe that was what my leg muscles needed. Moreover, doctors had advised yoga since they believed I was stressed and imagining the pain. Yoga is known to decrease stress, improve clarity of thought, and perhaps could reduce my so-called imaginary pain.

∼

We were staying in the officers' mess in Altinho, a hill neighbourhood of Panaji, the state capital of Goa. Attached to the mess was the Goa police gym – one of the best fitness centres in the city. All officers, irrespective of service, came to this gym, located on the first floor. The ground floor housed the yoga room, a large hall used for conferences and training sessions by the police officers. We had a well-trained yoga instructor, Mr Prakash, who had been coaching all the state's police officers for years. I introduced myself to him, and we decided to start training at 6:30 a.m. every day. Getting up was not a problem since I wasn't sleeping at all. So I was ready to go anytime he was.

The axe-chop pain in my groin continued to disturb whatever little sleep I got. In between these spells of extreme, agonizing, unexpected pain, I managed about two or three hours of sleep at best. As these axe chops continued, my insomnia worsened. I had started taking a stress-relief medicine and using an ointment. Three weeks after the pain first appeared, it suddenly vanished. However, my ankle and knee pain worsened simultaneously. My fatigue increased, and bending my knees became even more difficult. Sitting on the toilet was nightmarish.

When I started doing yoga, I faced even more problems. Bending my knees to sit in *padmasana* (lotus pose) was impossible. Sitting on the mat itself took at least a minute. I preferred doing the *shavasana* (corpse pose), hoping I could at least get some sleep during that time. But the sleep goddess was still unhappy with me – I was perpetually tired, and there was no respite.

After trying to run in the morning – which, by now, had become walking because of tiredness – I would go for yoga. Prakash would say, 'Sir, your body is very rigid.' In the initial days, I didn't tell him about the pain. I did *pranayama*, *anulom-vilom*, *bhastrika* and other exercises. After almost two weeks, I continued my practice, but there was no improvement in my condition.

Yoga and the stress-relief medicine had become part of my routine for two weeks. Though I felt mentally relaxed, I was physically exhausted.

∾

For my birthday, we decided it was time to replace my worn-out running shoes – it had been three years since I had bought them. Despite running almost daily and racking up 2,000 kilometres, as tracked by my running app, I had continued using the old pair long past their prime, mainly because the lockdown during the pandemic prevented me from shopping for new ones.

Now that it had been confirmed that my pain was psychological, I was keen to get back to my life as I used to live it. After all, I didn't have any problems; it was all in my mind. We headed to the Skechers store. But as we approached it, fatigue overwhelmed me. I felt so exhausted that the thought of leaving the car seemed monumental. Remya, frustrated by my lack of energy, questioned sharply, 'What is your problem? If you wanted to sleep or sit in the car, we could have just stayed at home.' I could barely stand; all I wanted was to crawl back into my bed. I didn't want to go to the shop. Once inside, I started looking for a chair to sit on rather than browsing the shoes. The fatigue made me feel as though my spirit wanted to leave my body. That day, I truly realized what fatigue meant – extreme fatigue. After we came out of the shop, having bought a pair of shoes, I just wanted to return to my room and sleep. Remya and the kids wanted to visit some other shops as well, but I insisted we go back home. Once in our room, I lay flat on the bed, completely exhausted.

I closed my eyes, begging God to allow me *some* sleep. I desperately wanted to sleep. But sleep was out of reach. It seemed angry at me. Exhaustion, sleeplessness and pain in my ankle, knees and fingers were taking over my life. Above all, the one thing I couldn't tolerate was insomnia. I reached out to Dr Benz and Dr Warrier, seeking any remedies or medicines that could help. Dr Warrier once again insisted I undergo a detailed check-up; Dr Benz suggested I give some time for the relaxation tablets to work. He also believed my lack of activities and assignments was contributing to these issues – I was too idle.

~

After a long wait of over a month, I was finally assigned my new role as SP (Superintendent of Police) at the headquarters. It wasn't a field position, but the workload was immense. Goa, with its two districts, has a much smaller police force compared to other states. Unlike places like Delhi, where there are around three to four SP headquarters, Goa has only one, resulting in a high workload. I had a very hardworking boss who had many plans for the furthering of the department. The work timing was generally from 10 a.m. until 6 p.m. With a workaholic boss, I also had to stretch my hours. But I loved the job.

Since I was getting no sleep, there was no waking up either – rather, after a sleepless night, I would start my day around 5:30 a.m. I went for a run, which, due to the knee and ankle pain, became a walk. Forty minutes later, I attended yoga, where I would flop onto the mat like a bag, hardly able to fold my knees.

After returning to my room, I faced two more difficult tasks in order to get ready: buttoning my shirt and pants, and having breakfast. Finer finger movements had become extremely painful by now. On most days, there was either *paratha* or bread-omelette for breakfast at the mess, neither of which I enjoyed every day, as a Keralite. Sometimes, tearing the paratha was so difficult that I had to ask the cook to cut it for me. My eye had developed a permanent reddish hue, and under my eyes, dark circles formed, which I attempted to cover up with talcum powder.

Around 10 a.m., I headed to my office at the Goa Police headquarters in Panaji City. The building, a relic from the Portuguese colonial era, housed the officers on the first floor. With the lift under construction, accessing our offices meant climbing huge steps – each nearly a metre tall. Climbing these steps daily was challenging, but coming down them was even more painful. In the evenings, the pain in my knees and ankles was so severe, it made me dread the journey home.

Since I was at the headquarters, there were frequent meetings with senior officers, all of whom had offices there. Everyone had some or the other work with me, so I would have to keep moving around. I kept a pedometer on me. There were days when I walked 6,000 steps within the workplace alone, shuttling between my office, the conference halls and the offices of the DIG (Deputy Inspector General), IG (Inspector General) and DGP (Director General of Police). Soon enough, the Christmas season came and went, ushering in a new year filled with fresh hopes.

# 2

As the first wave of the Covid-19 pandemic began to subside, with fewer curfews and lockdowns, we started to explore Goa, a prime tourist destination. Bored of the food at the mess, we started ordering food or going to restaurants once every three days. However, I soon developed a severe burning sensation in my stomach after eating curries and spicy starters. Despite dining only at top-rated restaurants, I struggled with the food. This discomfort extended even to the mess canteen's curries and fish fries; eating felt like swallowing acid.

Around this time, the renovation of our quarters was about to be completed; soon we would be able to shift into our own place. In just a few more days, I would be able to have good home-cooked food. I switched my diet to only bread in the mornings, rice and curd for lunch, and chapatis without any curry for dinner.

I started losing weight drastically. From 80 kilograms, I reached 76 kilograms within a month.

Initially, I thought it might be because of the change in my diet. Also, I was pleased as I had wanted to slim down for a while, which had proved extremely difficult after thirty years of age. Yet here I was, losing weight without much effort. I had heard yoga was great for weight loss but given that I had only started doing it a couple of weeks back, it was surprisingly effective for me. Encouraged, I decided to continue with my yoga practice.

Work remained hectic. From ten in the morning to eight at night, I was at the office. Some days, it even stretched until 10 p.m. Because the work was enjoyable, though, I didn't mind the schedule. I noticed an intriguing pattern: in the morning hours, I felt no bodily pain. All the pain would subside unless I made specific movements – twisting my ankle, bending my knees or using my fingers. The pain-free period lasted from about 7 a.m. to 12:30 p.m. Although fatigue was always present, its intensity was lower during these hours.

I took this as a positive sign. What the doctors and others said had been correct, after all. Perhaps I had been imagining the pain, creating my whole ordeal myself by overthinking due to lack of work. The medications and yoga seemed to be effective. I felt like I was returning to normal. Even the 'axe chops' had vanished.

But the good thoughts didn't last long. The discomfort soon metamorphosed into a new force with more intensity. The pain-free period lasted only two or three days before the pain returned as a nightmare.

It took on a new form now – a new pain cycle. After a couple of days, at around midnight, slowly, pain started to return to my knees, ankles, wrists and fingers. After lunch – some rice and curd, the only things that I could eat – the pain intensified. By 5 p.m., it became extreme, and by nightfall, unbearable, accompanied by severe fatigue.

Sleep was still a distant dream. It had been nearly one and a half months since I had been able to sleep. For almost three weeks, I hadn't enjoyed a good meal. My weight had now dropped to 75 kilograms. The pain had become so unbearable at night that I started taking a heavier dose of stress-relief tablets. As soon as I reached home, all I wanted was to go to bed, but I would end up rolling around, hoping for sleep. Yet sleep did not come – only fatigue and pain. Sometimes it was full-body pain; other times, it was localized. Such intense, unbearable pain that I started praying for the duller full-body pain instead. This localized pain also varied in its manifestations.

By 12:30 p.m., the pain first started in my knees, making it difficult to lift or extend my legs. Then my ankles would start hurting, though it was triggered by movement. After lunch, my fatigue got so severe that climbing down the stairs at the police headquarters was a struggle, and I'd have to hold onto the support lever to descend. Noticing other staff members talking about my condition, I decided to stop going home for lunch to avoid the ordeal altogether. By 3 p.m., the pain escalated so severely that any movement became a challenge. My wrists were immobilized, and my fingers felt as if they were on fire.

By 5 p.m., the pain would cause me to tear up in agony. My three bosses at the headquarters frequently called for work or discussions, and each time it was really hard to walk. Walking hurt so much that by 6 p.m., I was limping. The tiredness always started around noon. I would eat just rice and curd for lunch, but it made me feel like I had eaten a lot and needed to sleep right away. However, the painful steps stopped me from going home, so I tried to close my eyes and rest while sitting. Though I felt so tired, I couldn't sleep. These ten minutes of rest helped a bit, but soon after, my body felt as heavy as stone, and I couldn't move at all. It took me half an hour to get moving again, and it was very painful. Once I managed to get up, sitting back down felt like an impossible task, and I needed help to do it.

∼

In Goa, we frequently welcomed high-profile visitors, including senior ministers and other dignitaries from the central government. My boss, who took security duties very seriously, insisted that a senior officer be present at all times. As a result, I was often assigned to manage security and protocol at the airport. Although the job wasn't particularly challenging, it required extended periods of standing, which became increasingly difficult for me. During the first visit, I managed to cope, but by the third duty, I nearly collapsed and couldn't stand at all. As the dignitary passed, I remained seated, prompting a comment from a security personnel, 'You are supposed to stand up, officer.'

By the second week of January, my condition worsened daily. The pain would start around 12:30 p.m. along with the great fatigue and become unbearable by evening, extending into the night. The entire night, I would moan and toss in the bed.

Despite the sleeplessness, I was out of my house by 5:30 a.m. every day. With much difficulty, I would attempt some stretching to prepare myself for the run. Running itself was relatively easier – I did not feel as much pain. But because of the fatigue and sleeplessness, I couldn't run more than 2 to 3 kilometres at a stretch. So, I would run for a bit and then slow down to a walk in between the short spurts. After that, I would try to do some push-ups, squats and planks, but the knee pain made them impossible. My ankles also hurt too much. One day, I felt myself struggling to stand after trying just one push-up, for which I had to tolerate the knee, wrist and chest pain.

After my workout, I would go to the yoga lounge for pranayama. My IG and other officers also participated. I always took a place on the mat at the back of the room so that they wouldn't see me struggling while they were all sitting in the padmasana. For me, leave the padmasana, even sitting was extremely difficult. But remembering the mantra from training – 'no pain, no gain' – I persevered.

Post-yoga, I'd go home for tea, and after a painful breakfast, head to the office. By the time I reached office, my pain settled down as if it was tired, too, and wanted to take a break. This respite lasted for almost three hours every day. Then it woke up again. Like many of us, slowly, as time went on, its energy levels would increase. And so would mine; then fatigue would step in as usual. It felt as if the pain had my lunch for its breakfast and got renewed energy.

When I took a pen to sign, my wrist hurt. When I stretched my leg, my knees hurt; when I walked, my knees and ankles hurt, and I was limping by sunset. By 8 p.m., the pain would peak and by 9 p.m., I would be forced to retire to bed. It would then spread to the entire body and destroy my chances at sleep, making me more and more tired every day. The sleepless nights were now full of pain as well. My entire body would hurt, as if sharp thorns were trying to pierce their way out through my insides. I felt like Bheeshma on his *shar shaiyya* (bed of arrows) from the Mahabharata. I would groan like a puppy the entire night. Since I didn't want to disturb my family's sleep, I started sleeping in another room. I would also have to visit the loo almost every hour.

The days when the pain localized in my neck or lower back were the hardest. When my lower back was affected, it felt like I was sitting on a fireball. During impromptu meetings at the office, which could last anywhere from ten minutes to over an hour, I would stand throughout unless a senior offered me a seat. Typically, we would all keep standing, driven by the hope that the meeting would end quickly, and wouldn't even notice how time would fly. But this became increasingly difficult to do on the days when my lower back was in agony. As the pain worsened, after a while, whenever I went to the boss's office, I would pull up a chair and sit without waiting for permission.

Then the situation worsened. The pain would persist, no matter whether I was sitting, standing or in any other posture. Except for the morning, two–three hours during every day and night became a trial. I quit my walks. Yoga was out as well; sitting on the floor hurt too much. Days at work dragged on, exhausting. Simple foods were all I could handle.

I spent the nights crying from the pain. That's when Remya knew we needed to see a doctor. The pain spread, seizing me all day. Hot water helped a bit. I would stand in the shower, letting it pour over me. The heat was bearable, the pain was not. Especially not in my back and neck. Some days, no position brought relief. Initially, the intensity used to reduce when I lay down. But soon evenings and nights were getting progressively hellish. By 7 p.m., any movement was a struggle. By 8 p.m., I was in the shower again, hoping the hot water on my neck and back would help. One day, I started bawling like a baby, and my kids and Remya were shocked and scared.

Remya immediately called up the general physician I had consulted earlier. He could hear me crying in the background, since the call was on speaker. But all he said was: 'Sir is imagining the pain. He needs more counselling than medicine.' His words made me want to retort with, 'O sweet, knowledgeable doctor, why would I imagine and create pain for myself? Is this nectar or a spa massage?'

I asked Remya to call Benz. He said I should come to Kerala right away. It was January. Police hardly get leave then because of Republic Day. And that year, with the president visiting Goa, I was even busier. But I planned to go over the weekend and be back by Monday. That night, the pain was so bad, I thought I'd pass out. It was real, and I was scared. I had to find out what was wrong. This was definitely not my imagination. Some deadly disease was eating away slowly at my body.

When the president arrived at the airport, my condition prevented me from performing my duties. His team noticed and remarked on my inability to stand. Once he had departed, I approached my boss, informing him of my situation. He was so concerned that he told me to leave for Kerala immediately. My train ticket was already booked. Getting from the airport to the train station was a one-hour drive. I was in so much pain I cried the entire time. It shocked my driver and my wireless operator, who expressed concern that this seemed like an emergency and enquired whether I needed to be taken to a hospital instead. The train was leaving late at night, so I had booked a room at the Madgaon Circuit House. The security work for the president had really worn me out. I could hardly sit or stand or do anything. When we got to the Circuit House, I held on to my operator, Venkat, to get out of the car. I could barely hold myself up. My back hurt so much, I felt like dying would be better than this pain. Rama, the driver, and Venkat were both taken aback to see how bad it was. Up to then, I hadn't shown how much pain I was in. That day, they really saw what was happening to me.

To my dismay, the room allotted to me was on the second floor. Close to thirty steps stood in front of me, taunting me like a thirty-storey building. I couldn't even climb two steps; I couldn't keep my legs straight. I was struggling even to limp. I climbed the stairs like a chimpanzee, with my legs bent, holding on dearly to the railing, crying. All the people in the circuit house came out to look at me in alarm. Venkat and Rama ran to offer their assistance but somehow, I finally reached the room on my own. I flopped onto the bed, but the pain would not let up. I fell onto the sofa next. I thought I was going to die. While I didn't have a problem dying, I prayed for a less painful exit. *God, please do not let me die a painful death.*

I called Benz and told him what I was going through. He recommended a list of painkillers, which Venkat and Rama ran to procure. I remained in my room, screaming in pain. Ten minutes later, Venkat called me saying that the pharmacy refused dispensation without a prescription, which added to the frustration. Benz then had to send over a prescription, delaying the pain relief further. It was another hour before I took the medicine, and another half an hour before it started to show its effect. They were the worst four hours of my life, but eventually, the tablet started working and I felt relief.

I boarded my train at night. As usual, my companions on this journey were pain, fatigue and insomnia. I reached Kannur, where Benz had a flat. At the testing centre the next morning, he wrote lots of tests for me, including 'AIDS', 'hepatitis' and so on. I gave my blood sample, after which Benz immediately took me to a neurologist. After hearing me out patiently, he said that it sounded like I was experiencing symptoms of arthritis. Next, we went to a psychiatrist. Two hour later, I came out with a prescription recommending a painkiller and a heavy dosage of anti-anxiety tablets. The medical fraternity still believed my issues were psychosomatic; that I was imagining the pain.

I couldn't blame them for it, either. My blood test results still showed that I didn't have any of the infections I was tested for. The doctors I met were all specialists – the best in their respective fields. All my parameters appeared normal, and it seemed more and more probable that it was merely psychosomatic. But there was one change this time. The doctors no longer attributed the source of my pain to be *completely* psychosomatic; they thought it could potentially be an onset of arthritis.

My family had a history of arthritis, making this diagnosis seem feasible. Wherever I was experiencing regular pain, like in the knees, ankles and wrists, there was swelling as well, and the pain cycle was similar to that characteristic of arthritis. There was no pain in the morning; it started in the afternoons and reached its extreme in the evenings – just like in case of arthritis.

A good rheumatologist had recently returned to Kannur in Kerala after practising abroad. He happened to be out of station on that day, so we decided that once he was back, after two weeks or so, we would consult him as well.

Finally, I had an answer. It was arthritis. I got painkillers and sleep medication and had no other infections or diseases. I had not told my parents about my trip to Kannur. Nor had I paid them a visit. I was there only for a weekend – going on a Saturday and returning the next day. Whatever it was, I was now at peace with the diagnosis. While I was too young to have arthritis, at least the problem was clear.

I returned to Goa feeling satisfied. We had shifted into our new quarters as well by then, so my diet also improved, although I still struggled to eat spicy foods. After two months of enduring extreme pain and insomnia, I started to feel better. The tablets had an immediate effect. Within two days of taking them, I was sleeping again. Since I knew when the pain would hit me, I timed my medicines in advance. With improved sleep, my fatigue also began to reduce. Life began to feel more normal.

# 3

During this time, I had a lot of work and kept very busy. Some parts of my body still hurt. Specifically, a large lump on the right side of my upper neck, just above the medulla oblongata, which had been present for almost a year. I had shown it to the doctors, who said it was harmless, so I need not worry about it. But now it had begun to cause pain, though it was bearable compared to what I had previously experienced.

The other part that hurt was my left thigh. The painkiller had reduced all my other pains, but it had failed to alleviate the shooting pain here. It felt like axe-chopping pain, except that it was very localized. At one point on my left thigh, I felt a piercing pain, which was bearable except when I tried to sit. Another interesting new development emerged: My arms and legs started itching a lot. For this, I got an itching ointment, resolving this problem as well. Life seemed near-normal.

I started concentrating more on work. In the evenings, if I got home early, I taught Niya the alphabet. I slept properly. The swelling, too, had reduced. There was still some light pain in my wrists. I also started eating good food, but unfortunately, my weight did not increase. It touched the lowest point it had ever reached in my adult life, as far as I could remember. It was close to 70 kilograms now. At the police academy, where most of us reached our lowest weights, I weighed 74 kilograms. But now, without any effort, it had dropped to seventy-two.

After three weeks on the new medication, I took another three-day leave to visit Kannur for further check-ups. I was feeling pretty much fine now. I had started reading up on arthritis, and while there was no cure for it, there were several ways to cope with it. What I didn't like was the prospect of being on medication for the rest of my life. Yoga and meditation came highly recommended for managing the symptoms. They had significantly helped my mother throughout her twelve-year struggle with the disease. Her life was relatively normal, except during winters when her fingers and toes would hurt, even necessitating a minor hand surgery once. She had practised yoga regularly for a long time, which really helped her with the pain, and could now guide me. In any case, I preferred arthritis to the severe 'psychosomatic, self-imagined' pain and insomnia.

The airport at Kannur had recently become functional, and a direct flight now ran from Goa to Kannur. I arrived on a Saturday evening and immediately called Benz. He urged me to not waste any time and proceed directly for some tests he had arranged at a local lab. His vehicle picked me up and took me there.

This time, there was a particularly unusual test: I was handed a small can, typically used for storing oil, to collect my urine over the next twenty-four hours. This meant I had to carry it with me wherever I went during that period.

I had informed my parents about my visit, and they were eagerly awaiting my arrival. To prevent them from worrying, I initially told them that traffic delays would make me late. However, when I reached home looking gaunt and carrying a can of yellow fluid, their shock was evident. My father, who usually doesn't comment on my appearance, was visibly disturbed this time. He took my hands and asked, 'What happened to you? Why are you so thin? Your hands are very skinny.' My mother was equally shocked. Eventually, I admitted that my delay was due to undergoing medical tests to find out what was wrong.

Without further explanation, I went upstairs to my room. Soon after, Benz called, asking to meet him that afternoon since the rheumatologist was in town. During lunch, I told my parents that I might have arthritis and had to get some tests done to confirm the diagnosis.

My parents were not in the right state of mind to know what to do. They insisted on accompanying me. We went to Benz's clinic and waited there. That evening, I met with both the rheumatologist and the neurologist I had seen earlier. Being close friends of Benz, they conducted thorough check-ups. After discussing my symptoms for nearly two hours, the rheumatologist felt they resembled arthritis. He suggested steroids as the most effective treatment, promising immediate relief.

My mom, with twelve years of experience managing arthritis, became quite vocal when the topic arose. Before making his final diagnosis, the rheumatologist recommended a bone MRI of my upper back, as a couple of blood test parameters appeared slightly abnormal. He explained that the MRI would help ensure there were no issues with my spinal cord.

Benz fixed my MRI appointment for the next morning, near his clinic. The funniest thing about this period was the urine can. Over these two days, the urine can had drawn some attention, so I covered it the next day for discretion.

I went alone to the scanning centre, wondering why the doctor had said that the parameters did not add up. Wasn't it arthritis? Suddenly, out of nowhere, a question came to my mind: Was it really cancer? I didn't have any infections, so it was more likely to be arthritis, in my view. But what if they were wrong? What if it was cancer?

Holding the urine can, I entered the lab where Benz had informed them of my arrival. As soon as I entered, they called me in. Lying down in the MRI machine, I was moved inside. MRI scans are lengthy, and little did I know, I was entering a new phase of frequent medical interventions. Despite the doctors' assurances, I had a nagging doubt that it wasn't arthritis. I even started to fear that cancer might be the cause of my symptoms. After the scan, I hurriedly changed back into my clothes and, unable to contain my anxiety, asked the receptionist, 'What does the scan say?'

She said I could go inside and ask the radiologist – a liberty allowed because I was a friend of Benz's. Anxiety surged through me and I could feel my heart rate increasing. 'What is it, doctor?' I asked the radiologist. Without looking into my eyes, he said, 'You have to consult your doctor with the report. They will tell you.' Generally, if nothing appears adverse, the lab technicians and radiologists immediately tell patients that nothing is wrong to ease their worry. His reluctance to comment made it clear to me that something *was* wrong. Without hesitation, the words slipped out of my mouth: 'Doc, is it cancer?' His eyes were wide in surprise as he responded. 'It's not confirmed yet, but it does seem like it. You have big lumps in your body, very clearly visible around your neck. Your doctor will be able to tell you more. But it looks like cancer. I am sorry.'

Surprisingly, I felt both relief and sorrow simultaneously. Sad, because it seemed I was on the path to becoming a cancer patient, yet relieved that I might finally understand the cause of my suffering.

I returned home still carrying the urine can, said nothing to anyone, ate, and slept peacefully. Around 3 p.m., Benz called. He simply stated he would visit in the evening without further details. A prominent gynaecologist in Kannur district, he seldom made house calls. If he was willing to travel nearly an hour to see me, the situation must be grave. My fears seemed increasingly justified.

That evening, he asked me to meet him at the Rotary Club in Thalassery, a city in Kannur district. There, he greeted me and we walked up to the first floor. As we climbed the stairs, I couldn't help but ask, 'Bro, is it cancer?' His face filled with a mixture of surprise and sadness as he confirmed, 'It's not yet definitive, but it's likely cancer.'

On the first floor, he introduced me to his friend Santosh, a businessman who owned a resort in Munnar. Over whiskey, Benz shared that it was almost certain I had cancer. However, we still needed to confirm medically that the primary symptoms were that of lymphoma, which could be broadly divided into two categories: Hodgkin's and non-Hodgkin's, each with hundreds of subtypes. The next step was a biopsy to definitively determine if it was cancer. He mentioned there was still a slim chance it could be something else. The biopsy was urgent.

I was okay. I was calm. This surprised him. Generally, people react differently. He kept checking if I was really okay. I assured him I was cool – ready for anything. Then, he presented me with a tougher issue: How would I break the news to my parents? Given my mom's sensitive nature, we feared she might collapse upon hearing it. We sat there, thinking about how to tell them while sipping whiskey, and finally came up with an idea.

Together, we went to my house. Mom and Dad knew Benz very well. He did all the talking. He delicately explained how my symptoms indicated cancer and that a biopsy was needed to confirm. 'Nidhin is already low in spirit and depressed after the diagnosis. As his mom and dad, you need to remain strong and offer him good support during this period.' They were shocked, but the way things were put before them worked wonders. They even consoled me when I thought I would have to be the one to do so. I felt really proud of their strength and response. I also called Remya and handed the phone to Benz. He explained the situation to her as he had to my parents – I was depressed and needed her strong support. Everything was handled tactfully.

The next day, I checked myself into the Malabar Institute of Medical Science (MIMS), Kannur, for a biopsy. The surgeon, another friend of Benz's, reassured us that it was highly unlikely I had cancer, but a confirmation was necessary. Post-surgery, they showed me the lymph node they had removed via a small incision in my armpit. It was stored in a jar filled with fluid, appearing as a soft, ball-like object that seemed ordinary to me. I had assumed a cancerous node might look dark, but this did not. They handed me the jar and samples of the lymph node were sent for further analysis to the Christian Medical College (CMC) Vellore and Baby Memorial Hospital in Calicut. We were told to expect results in ten to fifteen days.

The following day, I returned to Goa. My life continued as usual. But anxiety persisted. More lumps were appearing around my neck, and the pain in my thigh was intensifying. Biopsy results typically include a primary and a secondary report. Ten days later, the primary report revealed no signs of cancer, diagnosing reactive hyperplasia instead, which is not indicative of lymphoma. This was a huge relief to us all – it wasn't cancer. However, the pain in my left thigh sometimes became unbearable, especially when I shifted from standing to sitting; the sharp pain made it very difficult.

Encouraged by the primary report, we decided to take a short break and travel to Kerala to delve deeper into my medical issues. We planned only a five-day trip, packing just enough for that duration. Confident there would be no long-term issues following the reassuring primary report, and with Benz's assurance that the secondary report was unlikely to vary significantly, we felt optimistic.

On 12 February, we boarded our flight to Kerala. As the air hostess instructed us to switch our phones to flight mode, Benz's call pierced through the quiet moment. 'Da, it's cancer. It is confirmed.' With heavy hearts, we settled into our seats, the weight of the news Benz had delivered hanging heavily in the air. The words echoed in my mind, bringing forth unexpected tears. Sharing the news with Remya, her shock mirrored my own. The initial relief we had felt fell apart by the confirmation of lymphoma in the secondary report.

# II
# Treatment

# 4

'Why, God? Why me? Did I commit such a great sin that you gave me cancer? What did I do? Am I going to die? If I survive, will I ever be the same? I'll lose all my hair. What about my kids? What will happen to me? What will I say to my friends? What about my parents? Will they be able to bear it? What about the cost of treatment? Will I be able to afford it? Might I have to borrow money for treatment? Will the treatment be difficult? What do I tell my boss? Will I get leave? But God, why me? What did I do? Was I so arrogant? I have always tried to be good to people, tried to help everyone and tried my best never to hurt anyone. I was honest, sincere and committed to my job. I never took bribes. There are so many corrupt, bad, sadistic people – why do they seem to be happy, while you give me cancer?' Obsessive thoughts like these poured into my mind and plunged me into sleep until we landed in Kannur. When I boarded that flight, I had never thought that in a couple of days, I would be stuck in a closed room, isolated, shuttling between home and the hospital for a long time. Nothing could have prepared me – or my family – for this.

The situation was still grim when we reached home. My mom wore a fake smile. I think she was remembering what Benz and I had told her before the biopsy. I smiled and told my parents, 'Don't worry, we will fight this out.' I called Benz and asked him what was next. He explained the steps. In cancer, diagnosis is crucial. Many people live with the disease without realizing it and never receive a proper diagnosis. Once diagnosed, the specific type of cancer is confirmed. Following this, the stage of the cancer must be determined. Only then, based on the doctors' findings and the patient's health and physiological condition, is the course of treatment decided. Treatments vary and can include various kinds: radiation therapy, surgery, chemotherapy, stem cell transplant or a combination of these.

In my case, the first two steps were over – I had been diagnosed with cancer, specifically non-Hodgkin's lymphoma, Grade 3a. Now it was time to find out at what stage it was. For that, I had to undergo a positron emission tomography (PET) scan, which involves injecting a radioactive glucose into an empty stomach. Cancer, being fast-reproducing, consumes more glucose than any other body part. In fact, it is because cancer eats up all the glucose that other bodily organs don't get any. I also think it is the reason one loses weight and feels immense fatigue when they have cancer. Once the radioactive glucose is consumed by the cancerous tissue, after an hour, the radiation emitted by these tissues is caught by the scanner. The scan shows the cancerous tissues and their activity level – the speed at which the cancer is growing – using which the doctors estimate the cancer's stage.

To my knowledge, there was no PET scan facility available in my locality, so we decided to go to Baby Memorial Hospital (BMH) in Calicut. My friend Ajay was working there as a doctor in the paediatric wing. The day before we planned to go for the scan, Benz and I discussed chemotherapy. I was very depressed and saddened that I had got cancer at a young age. That's when Benz told me that nowadays, many young people were getting diagnosed with cancer. He then revealed that Arjun, one of our mutual friends and my age, had just recovered from classical Hodgkin's lymphoma.

I called up Arjun. He and I were classmates from fifth to tenth grade and also friends with Benz. He had been cured almost a year ago, meaning he had been diagnosed at a younger age than me. An extremely lean fellow, though very intelligent and strong. During a medical check-up for the renewal of his health insurance, his company found something unusual in his chest. He was diagnosed with classical Hodgkin's lymphoma, underwent chemotherapy and was cleared of cancer. Six months after the treatment concluded, the cancer resurfaced – a relapse.

Looking at my shocked face, Benz said, 'Jolly, cancer hangs like Damocles' sword over your head throughout your life.' After the relapse, Arjun had to undergo a bone marrow transplant. It took one and a half years after that for him to rehabilitate and return to a normal life. I imagined Wolverine in the *X-Men* movie, when liquid metal adamantium had been injected into his bones. That's how he had got his shining claws. I remember how he cried and fell unconscious during that process. Wolverine, who didn't feel pain ... then I imagined Arjun as Wolverine. After a while, I saw myself as Wolverine.

Arjun asked, 'What about kids?' I said I had two. He said I had nothing to worry about in that case. The next question I asked was, 'Will stuff stop working?'

'What do you mean?'

'I mean if that is the case, then I would rather live with cancer than undergo treatment.'

He laughed and told me to calm down, assuring that nothing of the sort would happen. Everything would still work, but sperm mobility could be lost, making it difficult to have kids for some time after the treatment. Since I already had kids, I had nothing to worry about. He then advised me to wait until the scan was over before making further plans.

Arjun had undergone treatment at Christian Medical College (CMC) Vellore, so I decided to get treated there too. Benz agreed with this plan. Before that, Remya and I went for my PET scan at BMH Calicut early the next morning. Due to the pandemic, we travelled in our own car with a hired driver. Ajay had arranged everything for us at BMH. We met him and headed to the scanning centre.

While waiting for the scan, I met a middle-aged lady. She was from Malappuram and was accompanying her husband, who had to undergo the scan as well. He was already undergoing treatment for stomach cancer and they had come to check on his progress. He was a daily wager, a hardworking chap. More than 6 feet tall, he used to be hefty, when all of a sudden, he started losing weight and feeling more and more tired. He couldn't eat. They went from doctor to doctor until finally, he was diagnosed with stomach cancer. He underwent surgery and was now receiving chemotherapy. The mounting treatment expenses were a significant problem for them. 'Cancer treatment is extremely expensive,' she said. Everyone had abandoned them; it was only because of some altruistic religious organization that they had been able to hold up.

A nurse came and told her that she could go. Before leaving, the lady looked at me and said, 'Son, whatever happens, never let your mind give up. Cancer is a fight with yourself. The moment you give up in your mind, cancer will completely eat you up. And if you don't give up, then half the fight is won. Be strong. Be bold. That's the only way to deal with this disease. May God bless you and may you have a good and fast recovery.' Her words served as a beacon of hope throughout my fight.

For the PET scan, I had to be on an empty stomach. At the centre, they gave us a bottle of water filled with some solution I was required to drink. Then we had to wait for an hour, after which I was taken to a big scanning machine and asked to lie inside it. The machine kept turning around me and I kept moving inside and outside it. I was instructed from time to time to hold and release my breath.

After one round of this, a liquid was injected into my veins. The nurses warned me that it might be painful, but it wasn't. Instead, it felt warm. I could actually feel the hot liquid moving through my arms and all over my body. It was most noticeable in the groin, armpit and chest areas. Then began another round of moving inside and outside the machine, after which I was allowed to go. We had to wait outside for an hour until the radiation concentration in my body reduced.

Ajay had told me to bring the biopsy slides along the next time I came, to collect the scan report. He introduced me to the cancer specialist at BMH. The specialist acknowledged that while CMC was good, the hospital only allowed one person to accompany the patient at all times. During cancer treatment, the patient – me – would need family support, which would be very difficult to provide if I were far from home. Cancer treatment takes a long time, and if it wasn't institutionalized, i.e., if I wasn't an inpatient at the hospital, travelling back and forth would be challenging. He reassured me that BMH Calicut had the best cancer treatment facility available in Malabar (North Kerala), so I should seriously consider undergoing treatment there.

On my way back, I checked up on CMC and found that travelling to there was going to be very difficult for me from my home. So now, BMH was my only option. There was an MVR (M. V. Raghavan) cancer centre in Calicut as well, specializing in cancer treatment and another viable option. But at MVR, I wouldn't have any close friends like Ajay to support me.

I called up Arjun to ask for his opinion. He told me about his chemotherapy journey. He underwent chemo in a private hospital in Bangalore, and after it was completed, he was certified as cancer-free. He was asked to come in for follow-up check-ups. Six months after chemo, it was at a follow-up check-up that he found out the cancer had relapsed, after which he had to undergo a second round of chemo followed by a bone marrow transplant. The latter procedures were both conducted at CMC Vellore. During his treatment in Bangalore, he had called his parents to stay with him. While getting treatment in CMC Vellore, however, he ended up travelling a lot between Bangalore and Vellore. During chemo, the body's immunity drastically reduces, making the patient very susceptible to infections. And he used to drive to CMC Vellore along with his wife for his chemo sessions.

As Arjun started telling me more about the difficulties of undergoing chemo, he emphasized that I couldn't be alone during the treatment. Moreover, my food habits would also change during chemo. Patients tend to find food tasteless and don't feel like eating. At the same time they are supposed to eat more, particularly protein-, fibre- and nutrient-rich foods, which are ironically not as tasty as carbohydrate-rich foods. For better safety it's advisable to eat home-cooked food, which would become yet another concern. Due to these reasons, perhaps CMC wasn't the best option because it was too far and we were still in the clutches of the pandemic. Realistically, BMH was my only option. Arjun recommended I wait for my scan results before making the decision.

After two days, we returned to BMH for my results. I was in for a shock. I had stage-4 cancer.

There was not a single area of my body to which it hadn't spread. From my knee to my neck, it was everywhere. They had found enlarged lymph nodes in both my stomach and kidneys. The lymph node in my thigh was in fact so large that it was causing severe pain, which I had described earlier. The cancer had spread to the bone marrow, too.

Ajay took me to the haemoto-oncologist, a physician who specializes in blood diseases and cancers, we had consulted two days back. He advised me to get admitted immediately. Most probably, I would have to undergo a combination of surgery and chemotherapy. I asked him about the expenditure. He didn't give me an exact amount but asked me whether I had health insurance and was covered by the Central Government Health Scheme (CGHS), a healthcare scheme for serving and retired central government employees and their dependants. If so, there was nothing to worry about.

I collected my reports and told the doctor and Ajay that I would take some time to make my decision and inform them both. We had gone to Kozhikode, a city along the Malabar coast, by car – it had taken me three hours just to get there, because of the traffic. I had hated that journey. Meanwhile, the pandemic was running rampant across the world. Road journeys in Kerala are always tiring and long, and the roads are narrow and crowded. I used the travel time to think about the money for my treatment. I checked with my staff in Goa about medical reimbursement and advances. The Goa government had issued separate guidelines for medical reimbursement. Any government servant working with the state government had to undergo treatment at the Goa Medical College. If one wanted to undergo treatment somewhere else, outside of Goa, then they needed to acquire a no-objection certificate from Goa Medical College. I didn't have any of that.

When we left Goa, we hadn't expected to face such a dire situation. Now was not the time to think about expenses and reimbursements. I decided that first, I would get treatment; then, I would think about the cost. Life is the most important priority.

I called Benz. He confirmed that both BMH and the doctor Ajay had referred me to were good. By that time, the final report on my biopsy slide review had also come. I had Non-Hodgkin's Follicular Lymphoma Type 3, Stage 4. The doctor who reviewed my slide advised me to start treatment immediately. 'It is life-threatening,' she told me.

This was when I remembered my school friend, Mohan Kumar. Mohan was a tall, sturdy fellow who had been my friend throughout my childhood, till I passed tenth grade. He was the tallest in our class. In October 2019, when I met him along with a few of our other friends, he whispered into my ear that he had just finished his cancer treatment. I had asked him where he had been, as he had gone off the radar a long time ago. He told me about his testicular cancer and that one of his testicles had been removed. We didn't go into much detail then.

I called him up and told him about my case. He said he would come visit me at my home. During this time, I had also consulted a cancer specialist at Apollo Hospital, Delhi. He examined my reports and said I had to undergo chemotherapy. He suggested I consult Dr Chandran Nair, who had worked with him previously, and gave me his number. On inquiry, I found that Dr Nair worked at the Malabar Cancer Centre (MCC), Thalassery. The Apollo doctor had been full of praise for him, saying there was no one better than him for the treatment of lymphoma. Now we had one more option.

Mohan looked strong and healthy, showing no signs of being sick before. He told me he had surgery and chemo at MCC. He also said chemo was tough – it really wore on the mind and body. I needed to learn more about chemo, I knew. But I also understood that a new chapter of my journey was about to begin.

# 5

Every cancer requires a different combination of treatments. Similarly, there are also different courses of chemotherapy. Chemotherapy refers to treatment using chemicals. A combination of chemicals is injected into the body to target and destroy cancerous cells. Several doses are required because cancer cells are fast-reproducing. With each dose, the extent of cancer in the body is supposed to reduce, with the expectation that by the time the last dose is administered, all the cancerous cells in the body will be destroyed. If the body responds well (positive prognosis) to chemo, then generally no second line of treatment is required. In some cases, surgery may be performed first, followed by chemo to kill any remaining cancerous cells. Sometimes, radiation is used, too.

Since cancer involves genes, sometimes, even if the above methods destroy all cancerous cells, the DNA script of the body's cells may cause a relapse.

That is when there arises a need for a bone marrow transplant so that the cancer-scripted DNA can be replaced with cancer-free DNA.

Most cancer patients undergo chemo. The BMH doctor had advised I go for surgery and later, chemo. The Apollo doctor had prescribed R-CHOP chemo, a common chemotherapy combination that is used to treat non-Hodgkin's lymphoma using three chemotherapy drugs, a targeted therapy drug and a steroid. So it was clear that I had to undergo chemo. Chemo kills cancer cells, but it also kills all other fast-reproducing cells in the body. These include cells in the hair roots, nails, stomach lining, tastebuds and the food tract lining. All these cells are also burnt by the chemicals, leading to side effects in all the organ tissues made up of these cell types. There is hair loss – which is why cancer patients opt to shave their heads. There are also digestive problems, tastelessness and nail discoloration. Even the immune system is destroyed by chemo. Since my cancer had affected my immune system, primarily, the effect of chemo was expected to be cumulative, likely reducing my immunity to nil. For this reason, cancer patients are kept isolated from unsterilized environments. The first wave of the pandemic had just ended, but the infection was still present and vaccination had only just started.

Mohan told us that MCC had improved a lot since his time there. I had thought it was bad because of the stereotype that government hospitals are not good. He also reaffirmed that travelling to BMH for chemo would put me at greater risk of exposure to infections. During the treatment, there might be many complications requiring immediate and suitable medical attention. MCC was conveniently located, making it a very good option as familial and dietary support are easier to ensure if the treatment centre and residence are nearby.

Mohan also cautioned me that once people know about their cancer diagnosis, patients are usually inundated with advice from everywhere – the type of treatment one should get; the doctors to see; about non-scientific modes of treatment, such as *desi* and traditional remedies. He told me not to pay heed to any such advice as it is unscientific and potentially dangerous.

Just as Mohan had warned, once I started treatment, many people began giving me advice to try various desi remedies and even avoid getting treatment at MCC. Most of the suggestions about hospitals, doctors and alternative treatments were based on mere hearsay. Mohan advised me to listen only to the trusted opinions of two or three well-wishers and expert doctors, and to start my treatment. I was to remain positive and strong but also careful.

I was now convinced. I had taken the opinion of the Apollo doctor, who highly recommended

Dr Nair at MCC. I also valued the opinion of my dear friend and fellow cancer survivor, Mohan, who had undergone treatment at the same hospital. MCC was near my house, and considering the post-chemo side effects, it was easily the best option. I confirmed this with Benz, who told me he had undergone a one-year training in gynaecology at MCC and knew Dr Nair very well. He supported my decision, as did Ajay. Now I had to convince my parents.

The Malabar Cancer Centre was established as an exclusive cancer institute in 2001. It was hardly 200 metres away from my house, even appearing as the closest landmark on my postal address. We used to play in MCC's vicinity when I was studying in college. During those days, there was more staff at MCC than patients. It was a regular sight that the patients always returned dead from MCC in those days. But this was because then, MCC had only just been established and most patients were brought there only when they had no hope left and felt that no other treatment could save them – just to save money in their final days. That was the image of MCC I was operating with.

I had been surprised by Mohan's feedback about MCC. Repeated feedback from Delhi, Benz and other trusted people had made feel satisfied about my choice and proud of how far the local institute had come. This progress reportedly started after

Dr Sateeshan Balasubramanian took over as Director. When I was working in Delhi, around 2016, I had even called on him once.

My mom was very apprehensive about my choice. I was known in the family to be a miser and would jokingly tell my dad and mom that I was proud of it. My daughter Niya was delivered in Kannur Government Hospital. Naturally, they thought I had decided to undergo treatment at MCC to save money. But I stood my ground. Since I knew the director personally and had got good reviews from Benz and Mohan, my decision was made. I emphatically told everyone that they needed to respect my choice; I even had to raise my voice. By that time, we had started getting calls from the doctor at BMH Kozhikode saying that I needed to start my treatment immediately. The cancer had penetrated my lungs and bone marrow, and spread to my stomach and kidneys. By then, I had even started appearing malnourished. And my left leg had become limp. I was walking like a limp man. My left thigh was in a lot of pain and the lumps in my neck and head had grown, too. The lump on my head was so painful that I couldn't rest my head on a pillow. My parents entreated me to undergo treatment at a private hospital and offered to take care of the expenses. But I was set on my decision and decided to stick with it.

Before I went to consult Dr Nair at MCC, Benz came to see me. He called up the doctor and introduced him and I. Then he called the director of MCC, Dr Sateeshan Balasubramaniam. The next day, I got an appointment with Dr Nair. I entered the MCC compound – it was not like the old hospital from my college days. The number of buildings had increased, the parking lot was full and it was very crowded. There were a lot of people and lots of doctors. When I had last been to MCC, in 2004, the building had been completely empty. I remember the staff passing time talking to each other. Now you couldn't see any staff member idling around. They all wore uniforms – the doctors were in blue, the nurses in white and the supporting staff in green. All were busy with their work, running here and there. A lot of cancer patients undergoing treatment could be seen – easily identified by their fragile-looking bodies and hairless heads.

I searched for Dr Nair. Suddenly, I heard a voice. 'Nidhietta, why are you here?' I looked back. It was Shikha. She lived in my neighbourhood. The first time I had met her, she was a child. She was so cheerful and social that we quickly became friends. We used to play football in the MCC area when I was in college, and Shikha's house was close by. Every time I went to play, I would meet her and her parents, stopping for friendly chitchat. Now, after ten years, she was standing in front of me, and I was explaining to her how I had been diagnosed with cancer. She was sad to hear of it but reassured me that a lot of people had successfully completed their treatment and left the MCC healthy as they used to be before their diagnosis. When I told her I wanted to consult Dr Nair, she was even happier. She said he was the best and she happened to work as his assistant.

She took me and Remya to Dr Nair. Because of Shikha, from that day on, all our dealings with the MCC went off smoothly. Without much delay, we could meet the doctor. All of us were wearing masks, so I couldn't see his face properly; he sounded very serious and calm. I gave him all my reports. I thought after examining them, he would suggest I start treatment immediately. But he said instead that we needed to give the biopsy slides to the MCC lab and wait for their report. That was their protocol, and only after that could we begin treatment. I was surprised. The doctor we had spoken to earlier had told me to start treatment immediately, as if I was going to die if I didn't. And here was a cool doctor who calmly declared, 'We will follow the hospital policy.' I asked him how many days it would take, he said a minimum of ten. In private hospitals, it took up to two weeks – how could we expect it to be faster here, where the patient load was much higher? I was shocked. Had my decision to go to a government hospital been stupid?

Before leaving, I told the doctor that I had met the pathologist at BMH, who had advised me to start chemotherapy immediately. I think Dr Nair didn't like hearing that statement, for I saw his expression change, but he said nothing. Instead, he reiterated that we would follow the set protocol. He mentioned that the pathologist at BMH was his former classmate and that he would have a word with her, too. We handed the slides to the hospital lab and gave a blood sample for testing, then left for home. I immediately called Benz and apprised him of my interaction with Dr Nair. My parents were all 'told you so', and even Remya felt we should have continued treatment at BMH.

Benz told me that the slide report takes a long time to come, but he would talk to the doctor and speed up the process, and he would speak to Dr Nair as well. I felt like he, too, was sceptical of my decision. The next day, I went to meet Dr Sateeshan Balasubramaniam. Fortunately, he was available. He was already aware of my case. As usual, I went in limping and couldn't sit properly in my chair. He asked me what happened, and I told him I had extreme pain in my left thigh. He told me that once the treatment started, all the pain would vanish immediately. He checked my papers and said that considering my age, they would try to treat me with chemotherapy alone. If that worked out, there wouldn't be any need for other lines of treatment. For non-Hodgkin's lymphoma, R-CHOP chemotherapy was traditionally advised. He warned me that the chemo regimen would be extremely difficult, and I needed to be bold, strong and careful. I also mentioned the protocol issue, which he said he would discuss with Dr Nair and take necessary action. He added that he had directed the administrator of the institute, Mrs Anitha, to oversee my treatment.

That evening, I got a call from Dr Chandran Nair, asking me to come to him on the next morning. I called up Benz and he said he would come and meet me. He arrived by around 7 p.m., met my parents, Remya and the kids, before taking me out for a ride. I was finding it difficult to walk. We went to a bar and had a couple of whiskey shots. Then he asked me, '*Valsaaa*, are you ready for treatment?' I said yes. He told me again, 'You need to be strong, dear. The treatment is going to be difficult and long. But we are with you. Stay strong.'

I hugged him and said, 'Whatever it is, I am going to fight it out, bro. Having good friends like you is enough of a reason to live. We will fight it out, my man!' We both found it difficult to stop our tears from flowing.

We finished our drinks. During chemo, I was not allowed to consume alcohol. After the drink, he said, 'Now you are ready for chemo.' We both laughed.

It would be the last time I would drink, to this day.

# 6

The next day, Remya and I went to see Dr Nair. He was a man of few words. Thanks to Shikha, we were able to meet him without much waiting. Dr Nair examined my neck and thigh, where I had pain. When he touched the nodes, I screamed. He said it was the first time he had seen lymphoma with nodes that were so painful. I told him the pain had been much worse before, and there were times when I couldn't even sleep because of it. He checked my reports and told us that for non-Hodgkin's lymphoma (NHL), the traditional treatment was R-CHOP chemo. Considering my age, my body was expected to show good prognosis. Only if that didn't work would we have to try other modes of treatment. We were told we could start that very day. He prescribed some medicines, and Shikha took us to the chemo ward.

The chemo ward is a big hall with close to thirty beds. Beside each bed is a chair and an intravenous (IV) injection hanger. Due to the pandemic, every bed was covered by a cotton sheet, which was changed after each use. There was a security guard at the door. Outside the room was a long corridor with chairs for people to wait on – mostly cancer patients and their attendants. Most of the cancer patients were bald and had faces without a single hair. Some of them had wounds on their bodies created by cancer. The attendants, largely the patients' relatives, often looked very depressed. I think cancer affects your loved ones more than it affects you.

The process of chemo was as follows: once the patient had their doctor's prescription, they would have to pay the bill and get a coupon for their chemo. The first thirty coupon holders were allowed into the ward, turn by turn, along with one bystander. As soon as one entered, to the left was the pharmacy counter. One had to hand their paid bill to the counter, and the pharmacist would give them their medicines. Each patient received a big container of medicines. Then, they would lie down on one of the beds, and their attendant would go to the medicine-mixing chamber, where there were many paramedics. The attendant would hand over the box of medicines to a paramedic, who would take fifteen to twenty minutes to mix it into IV fluid, which was then injected into the patient through IV lines. The attendants had to sit in the nearby chair until the dosage was fully administered. Once it was done, the patient and attendant would leave the ward. The sheets of the vacated bed would be changed, the bed sanitized, and then the next patient would be allowed to come in and occupy it. This went on from morning to night until the last patient left. Almost thirty patients would undergo chemotherapy in one ward at a time.

The chemo ward can open our eyes to the extreme difficulties of human lives. Irrespective of age, everyone from small infants to octogenarians was lying on those beds, receiving chemo. People undergoing their second or third sessions were usually completely bald, even devoid of eyebrows. A fresh patient like me would look 'normal' as hair loss starts only after a few days.

Remya and I entered the hospital. Thanks to Shikha, we didn't have to wait long to pay our bill and get a bed. It was around 11 a.m. The chemicals were mixed, and it took another twenty minutes for the nurses to inject them. The pricking of the needle was very painful. The mixed chemicals were put into four pouches: one bright red and the other three colourless.

The chemo started with the red pouch. Before the session began, I had to take some tablets: one was paracetamol, and the other was to stop vomiting. Some older patients vomited even after taking the latter tablets. The first dosage began, with the red liquid entering my body in quick little drops. I tried to start reading the book I had carried with me.

The bed next to mine was occupied by a lady in her late fifties with stomach cancer. Her chemotherapy ended quickly. She was completely devoid of hair. Once she left, a mother and son occupied the bed. The kid was only around a year old. I started a conversation with them.

To our utter shock, the kid had blood cancer and was undergoing treatment. His hand was too small to take the intravenous injection, so he was given the medicines and chemo through his chest. The entire chemo ward fell silent, and the walls reverberated with the loud screams of this little child as the needle pricked his chest. I couldn't stop my tears from falling. All the other patients and attendants looked at him with sympathy, before returning to their own worlds.

Not a single tear was shed by his own mother. Strong as a rock, she held down the hands of her child as the nurses inserted the needle into his chest. The fluid started moving through the long tubes into the child's body, and after some time, the pain and the effect of chemo caused him to fall asleep.

My chemo had started to make me feel tired. To avoid boredom, they played Malayalam songs in the ward. Lulled by the music, most of the patients slept, and I did too. I woke up after an hour to find the red pouch had been replaced with a colourless one, which was almost finished. I didn't feel much difference except that the room felt hot, and I was sweating profusely. After the second pouch was over, they put on a third pouch. This time, the fluid was regulated, and the drops moved very slowly. My body started reacting. My saliva tasted bitter, like soapy water. I started shivering and getting goosebumps, feeling uneasy and sweaty. The drops were still very slow. The kid next to me had left, and an older person had taken his place. I wasn't feeling well enough to start a conversation. My mouth repeatedly filled with soapy-tasting saliva, and I kept gulping water to avoid those unpleasant sensations, but they persisted. The drops seemed too slow. We asked the nurses, and they told us it needed to be administered that way. If the drops stopped, we should report it to them. The room was getting warmer, and I dozed off again.

When I woke up, they were trying to straighten my hand. The drops had stopped moving because the blood vessels had twisted, restricting the flow of the medicine. This happened because I had changed my hand's position, and we didn't notice the drops had stopped due to their slow pace. Now there was a clot that needed to be removed.

To remove the clot, they had to take out the IV line and use a big syringe with a solution to flush the blood vessel clean. They tried to inject this fluid slowly, but it couldn't clear the path. The pressure then slowly increased, and I felt piercing pain as the solution cleared the clot. Almost every chemo session, I had to experience this pain. I always tried my best to keep my hand in the required position, but somehow, clotting always happened, and the clot always needed to be cleared using this technique, causing immense pain.

Finally, around 4:30 p.m., the third pouch finished. Now came the last pouch. The flow of the drops was better this time. By the time this last pouch was over, I was exhausted. My mouth was filled with a soapy but acidic taste, and my body shivered repeatedly, giving me goosebumps. I was one of the last people to leave the chemo ward that day. Mine was the longest chemo session of all. When I went to the restroom, my urine had turned completely red. The nurses had warned us of this earlier, so I wasn't surprised. They then told us to come the next day for an injection.

While I was receiving chemo, a counsellor came to us. She informed us of the side effects of chemotherapy and advised us to drink a lot of water and eat good food with less salt and spice. I was advised to avoid oily and fried foods and those that were not easy to digest.

I reached home feeling exhausted. I drank a lot of water and *kanji* (porridge) at night and tried to sleep, but I was feeling extremely nauseous. During the night, I vomited three times, ejecting lots of rice and chemicals. My throat was burning and dry. The exhaustion and the strain of chemotherapy ensured that I slept. The next morning, I was woken up by an urge to vomit. I ran to the washroom and vomited. When I cleaned myself and looked in the mirror, my face had swollen like a melon. For the post-chemo days, I was prescribed medicine for vomiting and a lot of steroids. I had to drink a lot of water. My mouth still tasted soapy, and I didn't want any food. I took some rice water in the morning. My food pipe burned when I tried to swallow, but thanks to the anti-vomiting tablets, I didn't puke it out.

The entire day was spent drinking water and lying down. The counsellor had advised us not to come into contact with anyone from outside. Visitors were not allowed. I was stuck in a room with a burnt food pipe, a soapy mouth, a swollen face and continuous nausea.

My face returned to normal size by the second day. For five days, I had to take only steroids. I drank almost six litres of water every day. Chemo was not as difficult as they had said. Eating was the hardest part. I was advised to reduce spicy foods, salts and oils, and eat a lot of vegetables. So from the next day on, I had food without salt or spices. It was tasteless. This was going to be my diet for the next three months. I had to push the food down. After I ate, I felt nauseous, which was my cue to take the anti-vomiting tablets. In the evening, I went to the hospital for an injection. This injection was supposed to increase my immunity. After chemo, I had to take steroids which suppressed my immunity, and this injection, known as a peg, was supposed to improve my immunity by artificially stimulating the bone marrow to produce more white blood cells. Cancer had already damaged my immunity significantly, and over time, chemotherapy was only going to destroy it further.

Until the next chemo session, I was stuck inside my room on the first floor of the house. I only came downstairs for meals. Every two hours, I was given healthy, tasteless food that had to be forced through my bitter mouth, down a burning food pipe, and I would have to keep drinking water. After two days, I started having severe hiccups. The hiccups were so strong that I felt like my stomach would come out of my mouth. I drank some water and they paused for a moment, before restarting. I made loud noises every time I hiccupped on the first floor, so loud that my mom and Remya came upstairs at the sound of it. My mom couldn't tolerate my discomfort, so she immediately called up the doctor and got medicine for it, which eased the problem.

I was just imagining how much my body was suffering because of all this intervention. First, cancer, then one full day of chemotherapy, which threw all my organs into disbalance and damaged them. Then tablets, lots of tablets, injections and even more tiredness – I prayed to God to give me more strength. Every time I was alone, my mind would start asking, 'Why me? Why did I get cancer? Why do I have to go through all this torture? At this age, I am supposed to take care of my parents. Now I have become a source of pain for them. Why, God? What did I do? Will I ever be the same? Will I ever get cured? What did my family do for them to struggle so much?' The mind created more problems than the body.

One good outcome of chemotherapy was that all my symptoms of cancer immediately vanished. All the lumps disappeared. The pain in my thigh vanished. The itching was over. I felt like before, except for the chemo side effects. Day by day after chemo, those effects also started vanishing. My hiccups decreased. The feeling of nausea decreased. The burnt food pipe started feeling normal; I think, perhaps, I adapted to them. For the first five days, I was on steroids. After that, until the next chemo, there was no medicine to be taken. The tasteless food and litres of water continued. I felt normal physically, though I noticed I was having mood swings. Once the cancer symptoms reduced, I felt calmer.

'Is this it?' I wondered. 'It's not as difficult as they say. I need not stay stuck inside the room.' I wanted to go out. My beard had started growing. My hair was not falling either. I felt confident about myself, 'I am a healthy person. Even cancer and chemotherapy can't shake me.' Because of the multiple warnings and the counsellor's advice, my parents and Remya didn't allow me to go out. I also thought I might be getting overconfident and should wait until after the second chemo to see how my body is coping.

Once I was stuck inside my house, my mind started playing games with me. 'What am I going to do? What am I to do the entire day? How long can I sleep? How long can I watch movies? How long can I read on my Kindle?' I started feeling restless.

After getting into service in 2012, I had always been busy. I had always occupied positions of responsibility where there was lots of work. Even the non-field posts had a lot of scope for work and serving people. I was always with people. I always heard people out. I always helped people out.

Now, all of a sudden, I felt lonely, unwanted, useless and like a liability. I wanted to talk to people, but what would I tell them? That I had been diagnosed with cancer? How could I tell them? I didn't want anyone to know I had cancer. People would look at me with sympathy and talk to me as if I was going to die. Thinking back, I probably hesitated to ask for help because of how people view cancer. I didn't want people to know I was undergoing treatment. My desire for privacy outweighed the need for reassurance and support.

# 7

During those first days, as I awaited the results of my biopsy, a moment of discomfort in a conference hall meeting highlighted the challenge of maintaining privacy about my health. Once, when the IGP openly inquired about my biopsy, I felt a pang of embarrassment as the topic of cancer dominated the discussion among officers. Until I completed my initial two rounds of chemotherapy, I resolved to keep my diagnosis to myself. Even in conversations with friends or neighbours, I avoided mentioning it, preferring to bear the burden alone.

To avoid confronting people, I stayed indoors, confined to my room. I didn't even go to the compound. I grew more and more frustrated. Especially five days after the first chemotherapy, it had become torturous. The question of 'why me' kept bouncing around in my head.

A week or ten days after the first chemo, I was returning to normal. None of the cancer symptoms were there, and the side effects of chemo had also vanished. I started feeling better. However, my food remained tasteless. The dieticians advised me to add lots of leafy vegetables to my diet. My plates were filled with leafy, spiceless, tasteless vegetables and very little other food. I felt like a two-legged cattle, sitting in front of my plate. I hated leafy vegetables except when they were made into curries. But I was supposed to eat plain, boiled leaves. How could I? There was no escape. With so much disgust, I'd push them down my half-burnt food pipe.

Before my chemotherapy started, we had sent our kids to Remya's parents' home. The doctor and others had advised that, because my immunity would be low, it was best to avoid any risks or exposure. The days started becoming increasingly boring and frustrating. Moreover, regaining a little confidence and health made me feel like the battle was already won.

I had been prescribed six cycles of chemo. Between the two chemo sessions was a period of twenty-one days. After the first chemo itself, I understood why. Chemotherapy causes damage to your entire body, which takes a week to ten days to recover. One had to keep drinking gallons of water to pump all the chemicals out. After the first ten days, the body starts recovering and by the twenty-first, it recovers enough to be ready for the next chemo, and then the cycle repeats.

Within ten days after my first chemo, I started feeling healthier. In fact, I was doing nothing other than eating. I missed my workouts. I even wanted to go for a run – that is how good I had started feeling physically. At the same time, being stuck in my room made me feel more depressed as well. I was expecting my hair to fall out, but that didn't happen. When I had left for treatment, my charge was given to my batchmate, and I was attached to police headquarters by the same order. The regained confidence, energy and health made me want to rejoin the force immediately. I called my bosses, and we discussed my return.

I told my boss I could rejoin and keep coming to MCC for my chemo sessions as needed. After each chemo, my body would take two to three days to recover, and then I could return to Goa and work. I proposed to continue this way until my chemo was over. The main reason for this was that I couldn't stand the depressive atmosphere, alone and without my kids around.

My boss told me to wait until the second chemo to decide. I even discussed it with Benz. He gave me some examples of people who were undergoing chemotherapy and going to work.

By the sixteenth day, I had completely recovered from my first chemo session. I had no symptoms. My hair was not falling, I could eat food properly,

I could sleep properly, except that getting too much rest all day made it difficult to fall asleep at night. I continued watching TV series and reading until I got sleepy. I just wanted to get back to Goa and get busy with work.

On the day of my second chemo, a blood sample was taken, and my parameters were found to be normal. My immunity was also normal. With little discussion, I was directed to proceed to the second chemo.

Like the first time, my session was the longest. Other patients kept coming and going. This time, a seven-year-old kid came with his mom. I saw him during the last hours of his chemo. I asked his mom about his case. He had a brain tumour, which turned out to be cancerous. It had been surgically removed, and he was there for post-surgery chemo. Seeing these children, I realized there was no reason for me to wonder why this was happening to me. The depressive thoughts about why I got cancer did not matter.

During this time, my family and friends also came up with different explanations for my diagnosis. My wife Remya said I was under too much stress at work. My mom said I ate too much non-vegetarian food. Some of my friends said I worked out too much. Others opined that I drank too much. There were a lot of opinions when, in fact, I didn't do anything too much. I still kept asking myself why. But after the chemo ward, I understood there was no point in thinking about that. What did the one-year-old child do to get blood cancer? What did the seven-year-old kid do to get brain cancer? There were pure vegetarians who got cancer, people in great shape who had cancer. When I asked Dr Nair, he said there was no specific reason, though there is a genetic component. But no one in my family had had cancer. The chemo ward taught me that it was just destiny. It's like what people say – everything that happens is already written. I was supposed to have cancer; to have this experience. If that was what I was destined to go through, then that's what had to happen.

The chemo ward also made me understand how easily hassled we humans are in our everyday lives and how trivial are the issues over which we bang our heads. In there were people with deep wounds. Those undergoing their twentieth chemo. Those experiencing the worst pain from surgery and chemo, or stem cell transplantation and chemo. If you feel consumed by thoughts about how tough your life has been, I'd recommend spending just two days observing the goings-on at a chemo ward in a government hospital. The pain and suffering alone will help you feel grateful for your blessed life. Everything else will appear too trivial to fuss over. The ward will bring about spiritual revelations.

After the second chemo, since all my parameters were normal the doctor didn't prescribe me an immunity booster. This gave me a lot of confidence. Perhaps I had won the fight after all. Now I just had to go through four more chemo sessions. This might mean I could go to Goa. I could rejoin duty and keep coming back for sessions. But when I asked my doctor about this, he told me to wait as he wanted to make his decision after observing my condition for a few days.

As before, the first three to four days after the chemo were torturous. But I think because of the confidence I had gained, I felt better. Or was it because of the hope of rejoining work? Whatever it was, the burnt food pipe, nausea, swollen face, tasteless food and drinking excess water all became more tolerable. A new side effect had started kicking in: constipation. I had noticed this even after the first chemo session but that had not been as intense as this time around. But despite all the discomfort, my anticipation of returning to Goa spiked. I was itching to escape from the confines of my room.

# 8

A week later, I called my boss, eager to get back to work. He was glad to hear from me but suggested I get the green light from my doctor first. My parents and Remya weren't happy about my decision – they thought I was rushing things. But nobody knew how hard it was for me to be left alone with my thoughts. I was determined to go back to work. And talking to Benz had helped strengthen my resolve.

At ten days, a new change emerged: I began waking up to find my pillow covered with hair. There was hair everywhere. When I ran my hand through my hair, it gave way without any pain or resistance. For the next two to three days, I had major hair fall. This meant my body had started responding to chemo. This was just the beginning. I was soon going to be taught a lesson for being arrogant and overconfident about my recovery. I needed to respect chemo; I needed to respect cancer; otherwise, they can break one's spirit, as indeed they broke mine.

After my second chemo, my confidence had increased so much that I had started going for a walk and a jog in the mornings. But not for long; just a couple of kilometres. I had been very excited. The only thing that made me feel bad was the hair fall. I had already trimmed my hair in anticipation of the hair loss, but since nothing had happened after the first chemo, I was confident my hair would be fine. But not anymore. I'd kill idle time by plucking out my hair from my head. Within a few days, my head started looking patchy, and the remaining hair started thinning, too. Benz and his sons had shaved their heads, and he asked me to follow suit.

Since I didn't like how my hair looked anymore, I shaved my head with a trimmer. And to my surprise, I didn't look too bad. I was happy. I had to shave every day; so I decided that once every two days, I would also shave my head once I returned to Goa. I was still adamant about going back. There was nothing else on my mind. There were heated arguments in the house, and everyone else was opposed to the idea. But I had decided, and all that was left to do now was to obtain a fitness certificate from my doctor. Then I could join work again.

I became rejuvenated by these ideas. I started going outside with my parents. I went out driving in the evening, just for a ride. I started behaving like a normal person, even forgetting that I was undergoing treatment at all. The new hope and lack of chemo side effects had bolstered my confidence. I started involving myself in all the affairs at home. Evenings, I'd take our car and go to the beach. I'd wear a cap to hide my bald head from the prying eyes of others. I started taking mom to the market.

One day, my dad wanted to buy a car washer; I also went with him. We parked the car some 200 metres away from the shop. The car washer was pretty heavy, so I thought I would carry it to the car. As I started walking with the car washer in my hands, I suddenly felt the urge to pee. It might have been because of the gallons of water I was drinking daily. But I couldn't control the urge, and that was the odd part. By the time I reached the car, I almost couldn't hold it in anymore. I put the car washer inside and started running around to find a washroom. By the time I found one, I had already wet my pants. I suddenly felt completely exhausted, much like in the initial days of cancer. Dad had to go to one more shop, but I told him I was exhausted and opted to stay in the car. By the time I reached home, I just wanted to sleep. Again, I felt an urgent need to pee. I reached the bathroom but yet again, I wet my pants. I couldn't control the urge or hold the pee in. I just fell flat on my bed.

Remya had gone to her parents' house to bring the kids back, since I had been feeling a lot better.

In fact, my plan was to take them along with me to Goa. I think my mom noticed I was tired and came to my room to check on me. She found I had a fever close to 101°F. She got worried and insisted I go to the doctor. It was around 6 p.m. I said the hospital would be closed and insisted we go the next morning. She kept pestering me to go to the doctor. I argued that it was just an ordinary fever from the exhaustion of the day and that there was nothing to worry about. I was worried, too, though. Not because of the fever, but because of the continuous need to pee. Every time I felt it, I ended up peeing in my pants like a toddler.

Suddenly, I got a call from Benz. Mom had called him. He asked me what happened, and I told him about the fever and uncontrollable urination. Without hesitation, he immediately told me to go to the hospital. I told him I would go the next morning. He said firmly, 'No, go now.'

That was when I understood the importance of proximity to the treatment centre. We reached the hospital in two minutes, by when Benz had called the doctor on call in casualty, Dr Nandini, another friend of his. She was about to leave the hospital when Benz called her. Because I was coming, she waited.

A blood test was done immediately as prescribed by my doctor. The report came in some time and showed my immunity was extremely low, less than

1,000. The minimum level is around 4,500, and for an average, healthy individual, close to 10,000. My immunity was badly compromised, and I had an infection that had resulted in a fever. I was asked to get admitted immediately.

Before admission, a Covid-19 antigen test was done. I was anxious about the result but, fortunately, was found to be negative.

Once I was admitted, they inserted the IV needle into my arm. Because of chemotherapy, my veins had shrunk and the nurses struggled to find a vein. With the needle piercing into my arm, this was very painful. By the time I finished my whole treatment, I had close to a hundred injection marks all over my hands. I still have those marks that make my hands look like a drug addict's.

Finally, they started administering injections to fight the infection and increase my immunity. I am still thankful to the nurses who took such good care of me. On the third day in the hospital, my neck, thighs and back started hurting badly. It began at night and continued throughout the day. I started screaming in my room. The nurses came running. I told them about the pain. They said it was a side effect of the immunity booster medicine, which activates the bone marrow to produce more white blood cells; this causes pain. And it was a hell of a pain. It did not subside when I sat, stood or lay down. After some time, another medicine was given, which slowly put me to sleep as the pain subsided.

Even after the third day, my immunity count did not increase. Everyone started getting really worried. At night, my lower back was racked by the pain from the injection. I kept changing positions, but the pain didn't reduce. I began to consider the possibility of death once more, thinking, 'My god, am I going to die?' The doctor had warned us that infections during cancer treatment can be life-threatening or even lethal. That is one reason everyone had advised me to go to a multispecialty hospital, where patients are kept under observation during the course of the treatment. All precautions are taken to ensure that they are not infected.

The pain and the closed room were driving me mad. In fact, more than the fear of death, it was the desire to die that had overtaken me. It had been almost five months of incessant torture and pain. I had just gained the confidence to try and get back to normal life; to do things I wanted to do, and life had struck me down again. But what about Remya and the kids? Who would take care of them? She had to have a job. After I die, she had to have an income. But how? She had left her job long ago, and we had planned to help her restart her career once we moved out of Lakshadweep.

She needed to get a job after I die. Who could give her a job? Karan was the best man for this, I thought.

Karanraj Vaghela, IPS, my batchmate. A Gujarati in the Gujarat cadre, he was the most resourceful person in our batch. He would go to any extent to help out his friends. We had our MCTP training together, just before I moved to Goa. His room was our *adda*. For any issue I had, I knew I could contact him and rest assured that he would help me out unconditionally. After MCTP, I hadn't called him. I didn't know where he was posted now. I called him, but he didn't pick up. I messaged him on WhatsApp that I needed to speak to him. He told me he was busy and thought I was joking. He didn't take me seriously, abusing me in a friendly way. I told him to call me when he was free the next day. I decided to tell him everything when he called.

'What if I die before he calls? Shall I drop him a message? No, he might be busy dealing with something serious. If I message him, I might disturb him.' From what I knew of him, he wouldn't be able to bear the sudden bad news. I still hadn't told any of my batchmates that I was fighting cancer. No way he could have known. 'Let him call. Then I will tell him.' But he never called, nor did I die.

The next day, my count started improving. Within two days, it reached 4,500, which is the minimum. After five days of battling with pain and staring into the face of death, I survived yet again. But I was shattered. My confidence was destroyed. I understood how precarious my life was. How unpredictable. I understood what chemo is and what cancer is. After I was discharged from the hospital, I was completely transformed. I understood the value of my health and body. How trivial a profession is, compared to one's health and wellbeing. How important it was to listen to one's dear ones rather than follow one's own thoughts and arrogance. I decided I would not think about my job until I was completely cured. Any small discomfort had to be immediately brought to the attention of doctors. I also understood how vulnerable I was. I thanked God that I was safe. I imagined what the situation would be like if I had been infected with Covid-19; I would surely have died. I thanked God for opening my eyes and bringing me to safety again.

As soon as I got discharged, my son Ishaan was infected with chickenpox – just as they were planning to return home to be with me. I missed my kids. I had ditched my plan to return to Goa, but I really wanted to be reunited with my children. Their company helped me pass the time and made me happy.

But now that Ishaan was sick, they had to cancel their plans. Remya also had to go back as well to be with them. My immunity was at its lowest as I was alone in my first-floor room, with my parents. Four more chemo sessions were left. Almost three more months. At least one month before the kids could come to be with me. I couldn't go anywhere. I couldn't do much of anything. What was I going to do with all this free time? How could I stop myself from getting more depressed? I decided to learn Arabic.

# 9

When I was posted in Delhi Police before moving to Lakshadweep, I had tried to learn Chinese. That was when I was in Jaipur heading the Delhi Police team doing recruitment for Delhi police constables in Jaipur. The recruitment process started at 4 a.m. and ended around 10 a.m. After that, there would be no more work for me to do. In those days, just to kill time I learned Chinese for three weeks. It is a tough language to learn, but I managed to pick up some words. And all the classes were online. My teacher lived in Bangalore, while I was in Jaipur. I thought of continuing my classes, but after I moved to the islands, I couldn't do so because there was no network there. Three years passed like three days.

I wanted to learn Arabic because I thought it might help me get a deputation in RAW (Research and Analysis Wing) or IB (Intelligence Bureau). I was interested in anti-terrorist operations, and I thought Arabic would be of great help. In fact, when I joined in Goa, I even searched for and got in touch with an Arabic teacher. Her name was Fathima. She was a Christian and knew Arabic, German and Portuguese. I had almost started taking classes with her when I faced the initial painful days of treatment. Now I could restart my classes. I called Fathima madam and told her what I was going through. She immediately agreed, empathizing as a cancer survivor herself. While working in Qatar she had been diagnosed with breast cancer and had to undergo chemo. She had also been stuck in a room for a long time. It was then that I understood how only a cancer patient could truly understand the pain of another. Others, I feel, can't help and just sympathize and forget. It is said nowadays that cancer is curable, but this doesn't quite capture the torture one has to endure throughout. The treatment can be long and devastating for the family. It breaks one's body and spirit and changes their life forever, negatively impacting mental health, family life and social interaction. It feels that one's identity is lost, as if one is plunged into oblivion.

Fathima ma'am agreed to hold classes in the morning from 9 a.m. to 10 a.m. Arabic was just as difficult as Chinese had been, but it was interesting. I found there were a lot of words in common between Arabic, Hindi and Malayalam. I started enjoying learning Arabic. After the class, I had a lot to revise. I kept myself engaged, studying Arabic the whole day. I became more and more interested and started taking lessons over the internet.

However, I was sleeping after lunch, making it difficult for me to sleep at night. To prevent myself from taking long afternoon naps, I arranged for one more class in the afternoon. Through one of my friends, I got Askar sir's contact, who was based in Malappuram. He taught me Arabic in the afternoon. Now my day was completely packed. From 9 a.m. to 10 a.m. was Fathima Madam's class and 3 p.m. to 4 p.m., Askar sir's. But I no longer had enough time to study. So I started getting up early in the morning, at 5 a.m. Slowly, it became a habit.

I completely stopped thinking about my job and Goa. I concentrated fully on recovering my health and learning Arabic; the near-death experience had made me understand why I needed to listen to my dear ones. No more adventure. I simply ate what was given to me, I didn't go anywhere. I stayed in my room, studying Arabic and attending my classes.

One change worth mentioning during this time was the shift in my diet. Before the hospital admission, my diet was full of leafy vegetables. My plate was heaped with greens. I was not given eggs, meat or any hard-to-digest food. Upon discharge, the dietician recommended I eat more protein-rich foods. So now my food had a lot of sprouted legumes. The leaves on my plate were replaced with sprouts. I was given boiled eggs, and once in a while, I also ate chicken.

Without much trouble, my third chemo session also concluded. This time, a three-year-old girl with liver cancer had come in. The staff were saying she would survive, though liver cancer is fatal. For half the chemo session, she was screaming in pain. The next day, I had to take a peg injection, which was to improve my immunity.

The chemo side effects were there, by now we knew how to cope with them. There were tablets for nausea and hiccups, and for everything except for my obsessive thoughts – which I controlled by keeping myself completely engaged in Arabic. From the third day after chemo, I had classes. By now, my son had also recovered from chickenpox and after getting 'Doctor' Remya's approval, I brought the kids to my home. After one and a half months, our family was finally reunited.

One of the worst side effects of chemo is the mood swings, which I didn't initially recognize. I thought I'd just changed mentally. I was a fairly composed person, never quick to anger. But during treatment, I started getting angry quickly and unnecessarily, and it persisted for a long time. One day, I blasted my mom over a small argument. My dad is a very nice, calm person. Once when he was unnecessarily checking the inverter, it caused a power outage. I don't know why that made me angry, but I blasted him, too. Marching around fuming like a mad dog, I started scolding everyone else in the house. For trivial reasons, I started getting angry at my kids.

One day, Remya told me to try and be calmer and do pranayama to relax. She said chemotherapy had worsened my temper and I would, one day, be destroyed by my anger. I remembered what the chemo counsellor had told us: chemo could lead to mood swings, and one had to be careful about their anger. I had depressed and angry days. I realized I needed to be more cautious about avoiding interactions that might make me angry.

So I stayed mainly in my room and came downstairs only to have meals. The children hung around me most of the time because they enjoyed it. Ishaan had been attending online classes because of the pandemic, but by the time he returned home, his classes were over and his vacation had started.

I took this opportunity to start teaching him Malayalam. To take a break from Arabic, I spent one hour in the morning after my classes on Ishaan's Malayalam tuition. Now my routine was as follows.

I would wake up at 5 a.m. and freshen up, then start studying Arabic until 8 a.m. Then I would go down for my morning tea and read the newspaper. At 8:30 a.m., I would have breakfast. From 9 a.m. to 10 a.m. was my Arabic class with Fathima ma'am. After that, I would go downstairs to have eggs, sprouts or milk for protein. At 10:30 a.m., I sat with Ishaan to teach him Malayalam until 11:30 a.m. Then I'd take another small meal, usually oats. After that, I studied Arabic again till 1:30 p.m., took a bath, had a sprouts- or legume-rich lunch and tried to take a quick nap before my next Arabic class at 3 p.m. The class went on till 4:30 p.m., after which I had tea and bananas. From 5 p.m. to 6 p.m., I either studied or walked around the compound. I prayed around 7 p.m. Then, daily, had some pomegranate, studied till 8:30 p.m., had dinner, and studied again till 10 p.m. or watched TV before sleeping.

Life had become tied to a schedule. The more I engaged myself in this routine, the less disturbed my mind felt. Otherwise, obsessive thoughts of 'Why me? What next? Will chemo work? Will there be a relapse? Will I have to undergo a transplant? Will I be cured? What about my career?' wreaked havoc in my mind. The saying 'An idle brain is the devil's workshop' is not a proverb but a postulate, in my view; a fact like water flowing from a higher elevation to a lower one.

Anger is difficult to control, often an offshoot of such frustrating thoughts. So how could I control my anger? By controlling my thoughts. How could I control my thoughts? By keeping my brain engaged. I worked hard to fill it with Arabic words, letters, grammar, rules and sentences, and continuous activity.

The days started feeling normal. 14 April was Vishu, the start of the Malayalam calendar year.

We Keralites start the day by opening our eyes to Lord Krishna, then burst crackers, wear new dresses and have a sumptuous lunch. The elders give Vishu *kaineettam* (money) as blessings. There is a belief that the first day of the year is an indicator of how one's entire year will go. I had already had a troubled year so far. I wanted the next year to be peaceful. I wanted it to be perfect – except that I was still under treatment for cancer. I went to bed early so that after Vishu Kani (first sight), I could study Arabic and stick to my daily routine.

By the time I had my dinner, I had developed a pain in my back. It originated at the tip of the backbone. I thought it might be because of sitting for too long; some stretching might help. I went to bed and slept. At 10:30 p.m., I was woken up by severe pain in my chest. It felt like it was being torn open; the pain was intense. I started screaming, but I was alone in the room. No one heard me. 'What is this, God? Is the cancer coming back? Am I having a heart attack?' I thought I would die. During my fight with cancer, I remember exactly four times I thought I was going to die. The first was when I had severe symptoms. The second was when I got an infection and had to be admitted to the hospital. This was the third time.

Severe pain like this was my first symptom of cancer. But this pain was different. It originated exactly in the middle of the chest and rippled to the side. I kept rolling around for hours, waiting for death or sleep. I checked the time. It was 2:45 a.m. I had now spent the last four hours in pain. I don't know why I didn't call anyone; it might have been because I didn't want anyone to panic or possibly watch me die. Extreme pain impairs a person's logic, and emotions take over. I was not thinking straight. With tears in my eyes, biting my teeth in pain, I was rolling around in my bed, waiting. 'Death, please take me, but let it be in my sleep.' I always believed there was no better way to die than during one's sleep. 'Please God, let me die in my sleep.' Suddenly, out of nowhere, I remembered the first day I had severe chest pain and had called Benz. That day, he had advised me to take paracetamol and sleep. I had a Dolo 650 lying in my bedside drawer. I immediately took two tablets and went back to bed, waiting for death in my sleep.

Around 3:30 a.m., my mom came and called me to see Vishu Kani. I woke up with a start. 'No, no pain in my chest anymore; I am alive.' The paracetamol had worked. I had slept, but the night had passed. I didn't tell anyone about how I felt. Although I was tired, I could not sleep, so I started studying Arabic.

Almost five hours later, around the time when I usually had breakfast, sudden, severe pain started in my back and lower waist. I could not sit. I took my breakfast standing up and went upstairs. Seeing me hold my sides and eat breakfast silently, everyone grew worried. On hearing about the pain, they suggested I call the doctor. I never rejected any advice from my mom or Remya, but it was still too early in the day, and the doctor wouldn't have reached the hospital yet. Instead, I went back to my room, took a Dolo 650, then waited. Since I hadn't slept the previous night, I fell asleep. After some time, I woke up to see Remya sitting near me, looking at me sadly. She told me to call the doctor. I called one of Dr Nair's junior doctors, Dr Unnikrishnan, who was a friend of mine. He told me the pain was because of the immunity-booster injection, peg. There was no solution – I would have to bear the pain. Only if I got a fever above 101°F should I go to the hospital. I had a mild fever of close to 100°F. He advised me to take a paracetamol tablet if the pain was severe and unbearable, which I had already been doing.

The immunity booster was activating the bone marrow in the big bones of my body, forcing them to produce white blood cells. This caused pain in my chest, back, thighs and shoulders. The big bones include the rib cage, the spinal cord, thigh bones and shoulder bones. It was the seventh day since my chemo, and the seventh, eighth and ninth days were hellish. The pain kept shifting from one bone to another. My hands felt so heavy, as if they were tied to dumbbells. As soon as the pain started, I'd take a paracetamol and sleep. Another problem was severe exhaustion. I couldn't get out of bed. Pain–paracetamol–sleep; pain–paracetamol–sleep was how my entire day passed. Paracetamol took half an hour to take effect and put me to sleep. After the three days had passed, the pain stopped, and I felt normal. For those three days, I couldn't do my Arabic classes, study or do anything. But the ten days that followed were normal, and then it was time for my fourth chemo. Before that, I had to undergo a computed tomography (CT) scan. The scan results were very encouraging; the lymph nodes everywhere had shrunk, except for a few here and there.

During my fourth chemo, I took my mobile phone with me to the ward, along with headphones, and put on a movie. Every now and then, I would fall asleep. When I'd wake up, I'd go back to watching the movie. When I felt the acidic taste in my mouth, I would start chewing bubble gum. Except for the occasional cries of a small girl diagnosed with kidney cancer, the session went off smoothly.

Though naturally, children cry a lot during treatment, I think God holds a special place for them. The hospital staff told me that nearly all of them survived cancer. Even Covid-19 didn't infect these children. As far as I know, cancer is not as fatal for children, except for the hardships of the treatment itself.

The peg injection was administered following chemo, as usual. Within two days, I restarted my classes and was completely engrossed in studying Arabic once again. I also resumed Ishaan's Malayalam classes. Six days went well but on the seventh day, the pain and exhaustion started up again. The pain was so terrible that sometimes I took two paracetamols to get relief immediately. For three days, again, I couldn't get out of bed.

Now I understood how my body was responding to chemotherapy and the cause of my pain. For five days after each session, I had to take steroids. Steroids suppress immunity so that it doesn't fight with the chemicals in chemo. Because of the steroids, the peg or immunity booster injection was also dormant. As soon as the steroid dosage was over, the peg started functioning. The bone marrow was activated, which resulted in pain and a hardness in the hands and legs. That went on for three days. After the tenth day, I was quite normal until the next chemotherapy session, which came after an interval of twenty-one days.

I understood I needed to take a break from my classes and routine on the seventh, eighth and ninth days after each chemo session. Other than that, I could go about my new schedule as planned.

By this time, word about my cancer had spread. Two of my colleagues from Goa came to know of my leave of absence, and slowly, the news reached other people who were trying to contact me. More of my neighbours came to know. More relatives came to know. I thought everyone would want to talk to me, but no one called. Maybe they didn't want to talk about it.

My neighbourhood friends, Sreelesh, Rajeesh, Mukesh and Rejil, came to meet me as soon as they learned of the fact. They made a lot of jokes and I felt great spending time with them. In fact, despite their limited knowledge, they did whatever they could to help me. Sreelesh had heard somewhere that sour fruit was good for cancer. So he kept sending me sour fruit. Though I didn't like the fruit, I couldn't help but accept it because he was sending it out of sheer affection. Shyjesh, another friend who ran a medical store nearby, gave me medicines whenever I wanted them. Mukesh, who worked as a police constable, assured all help if anything was required. They kept calling to ask after my health from time to time.

My office staff in Goa – Venkat and Suraj who were my wireless operators; Rama and Gauresh, my drivers; Kalidas, Prabjot, Sachin, Sumedh and Sai, who were my office staff – kept on calling me to ask about my health. Arjun and Mohan also did the same. I started feeling like there was no point in hiding my condition from my friends. The more my friends inquired after me, the more wanted I felt; the more motivated to win the battle.

# 10

During this period, one day, I received some sad news. My teacher from the tenth standard, Jayan Master, had passed away from non-Hodgkin's lymphoma. The news was circulated in our school WhatsApp group, prompting a discussion around it. Jayan sir had been diagnosed with NHL and asked to undergo chemo. But he was reportedly concerned about his appearance post-chemo and sought other options. The doctor suggested surgically removing infected lymph nodes, so he went ahead with the surgeries and thought the battle was won.

He went home happy, but after a few months, he had a relapse. Cancer, upon relapse, returns with double the strength, ready to kill. As a result, he was prescribed twenty chemotherapy sessions. By the thirteenth or fourteenth round of chemo, he was exhausted and tired of getting treatment. His advanced age, too, added to the severity of the problem. He eventually fell down, suffered an injury, which led to the wound getting infected. His body finally gave way.

I don't know what made me do it, but I posted, 'Same cancer, me too', and shared pictures of my bald head with the caption, 'fighting it out', in the WhatsApp group. Immediately, the point of discussion in the group shifted from Jayan Master to me. Most of my school friends started calling. Some of them saw my messages later and called or messaged the next day. That day, I understood how good friends were for one's spirit.

I had shared news of my condition only with Benz and another friend, Rony. From the days I first started experiencing cancer symptoms, I called Rony whenever I felt depressed. He used to motivate, inspire and guide me. Though he was a year junior to me in college, I always felt he had the wisdom and pragmatism of someone beyond his years. After the Jayan Master incident, I decided there was no need for me to keep my cancer a secret.

Every time someone talked to me and asked how I was doing, I would talk to them about my treatment openly. Though often, only sounds of sympathy and sadness came from the other end, I felt relieved. In fact, one visit to the chemo ward at MCC is enough to tell a person that cancer is very common nowadays. A few decades ago, it was considered a death sentence, but now if diagnosed at the right time, you can be cured fully and return to normal life. Since my body had, by then, started responding well to treatment, I also felt I was getting better. Though there was always going to be a risk of relapse and the treatment was exhausting, the disease itself is not as life-threatening as it used to be. And of course, proper diagnosis and treatment are essential for this outcome.

Once I started talking to people more openly, I was also flooded with unsolicited opinions and advice. 'You can go to that place, there is a traditional doctor there'; 'you should try Ayurveda'; 'there is a homeopathy doctor you should consult, who got famous after curing a lot of cancer patients'; 'Nidhin, you should have gone to that hospital'; 'you should have gone to that doctor'; 'I can fix an appointment with him for you'; it was endless.

Fortunately, Mohan had given me sound advice so early on. I rejected all the suggestions and offers. I was courageous enough by now to take on the world despite my condition. I didn't feel bad telling people I had cancer. I resolved that if I survived this, I would help others who were fighting the disease, too, by sharing my experience candidly. There is no need for anyone to feel depressed about getting cancer.

By the time my fifth chemo session neared, my body had started changing. I had completely lost my hair, including my moustache and eyebrows. I had put on a lot of weight. Benz had told me that steroids have that effect, and I was getting fat a lot faster; eating – or being made to eat – four to five times a day. I was sitting all day, and except for an evening stroll, got no exercise.

I also felt increasingly weak, tired, despite putting on weight. Even ten minutes of walking completely exhausted me. On the weekends, Benz would come to meet me. Whenever he came, he used to take me out. He was the only person with whom I was allowed to go. We used to go out once a fortnight, on a Sunday.

And recently, he had bought a Mercedes Benz.

I was the first person Benz took on a ride in his new, fancy car. But every time, even after taking a small stroll, I would feel completely exhausted. My body had become very weak.

By now, the second wave of Covid-19 was spreading like wildfire, and I hadn't been able to take even a single vaccine dose. If I were to get Covid, it was sure to be fatal. Once a person who could easily run half a marathon or swim 5 kilometres nonstop, I couldn't even walk continuously for ten minutes anymore. Cancer and chemotherapy had completely destroyed my body and immunity. I felt like a fat, ugly mass of meat with a belly and bald head, no eyebrows and no hair. The only way out of it was through focusing all my attention on Arabic. I didn't allow myself to sit idle for one second. I kept studying, writing Arabic, and memorizing new words.

Since I had started sharing the news myself, it had also started spreading faster. When Karanraj came to know, he simply couldn't believe it. I had to video call him so that he was convinced. He was a doctor himself and asked me to send him my papers so he could consult his friends. A day later, he called me again in tears, saying that I was a blessed man because I would have surely died if my diagnosis had been wrong or a little late. He gave me a surprise, too. Without informing me, he flew all the way from Ahmedabad, where he was posted, and came to my home. I was not only surprised but delighted to see him. He spent some time with me and returned on the same day. Before leaving, he hugged me and said, 'Nidhiney' (that's how Kerala officers were joked on by other state officers, mocking the way we called each other), 'stay strong, we want you back, we are with you. For anything, never hesitate to call.' He felt guilty about not returning my call on the day I was admitted to the hospital and messaged him to call, waiting for my death.

My Kerala batchmate Nooh IAS visited me. My Mussoorie roommate Ravishankar Shukla made sure to video call me every Sunday. My batchmates kept calling and enquiring after me. The more people called to check up on me, the more strength and power I gained to fight my cancer. If you know someone struggling with cancer, do not hesitate to call them. They may be going through the worst pain of their lives, but a sense of feeling loved and wanted in people's lives can offer a lot of strength. As the lady told me during my first PET scan, 'Sir, never give up; the fight is in your head.' The moment your mind gives up, your body can't do anything.

All this increased my urge to get my life back. 'Everything is going to be okay,' I kept saying to myself. The CT scan after the third chemo had shown a good prognosis.

I started thinking once again about going back to Goa. One more chemo. I just had to bear it one more time. I kept learning Arabic so that I remained engaged and the days went by faster.

When Benz came over one weekend, he attributed my potbelly and rapid weight gain to the steroids. Once the chemo was over and I was free of cancer, I planned to restart my workout and reduce weight.

Finally, the last chemo was also done with. A full day of chemotherapy, yet again. It was punctuated by the cries of a young girl who had eye cancer. She was wearing an eye patch. During the last chemo, the staff asked for my feedback. I suggested that infants and children be administered chemotherapy separately from adults. They should have their own chemo ward; it might benefit everyone.

After the chemo, the doctor asked us to meet him after two weeks. Maybe because it was the final chemo session, I didn't feel the chemo side effects as intensely. The same cycle repeated once more. But this time, even before the pain started, I took paracetamol tablets, which made the pain a lot more bearable. Though there was still exhaustion – I slept for the entire three days when it was at its worst – but this time, I managed to squeeze in one Arabic class.

Arabic kept me going till the day of my doctor's appointment. Now that the treatment was over, they were going to do a PET scan to see if it had had the desired effect. I was confident my cancer had been defeated, though the scary what-ifs still lingered in my mind. My CT scan after the third chemo had shown positive results, my body weight had increased, and I was feeling far better than when treatment had started. Moreover, I had followed all the instructions of doctors, dieticians and family members to the letter.

On the day of consultation, we went to the doctor with our hearts pounding. 'What will he say? Is everything okay?' Because of Shikha, we got an appointment quickly. Dr Nair didn't say much; he just complimented me for completing my chemo and prescribed a PET scan.

We went eagerly to the nuclear medicine area to get an appointment. When we reached, I was shocked at what I was told. They were going to do a PET scan only one and a half months after the last chemo session. That was their standard protocol. Further, they said they generally did it only after two months, but since I was young, one and a half months was enough time. I tried to argue with the nurse there, but she wouldn't give in to my requests. I felt angry, frustrated and sad. She gave us an appointment for 23 July – forty-five days after the last chemo session. But I couldn't wait one more day to get out of that hell.

Forty-five more days of waiting. There was no other way.

That's when Rony came up with the idea of me writing a book about my experience. He was very confident that I had already won the battle. During the five months of my treatment, I had understood a lot about the disease. There were endless stigmas, misconceptions and misunderstandings around it. There were also a lot of emotional, physical and mental hardships a patient had to endure while fighting the disease. More than the patient, his or her family had to undergo bigger agony. When I had started treatment, I too was totally unaware of what I would have to go through. It was only because of my good friends and cancer survivors like Mohan and Arjun, that I felt prepared for the battle that lay ahead of me. Being diagnosed with cancer can make one feel like an outcast. Especially after the start of chemotherapy with its side effects and the changes in one's appearance, it feels like you are being punished for your life's bad deeds. I had survived chemotherapy. I had hopefully defeated cancer. Now I was only one PET scan away from getting my life back.

Though the last five months had been very difficult for me, with the help of my family, my friends and God, who gave me strength and courage, I had withstood it all. I had reached the last phase of my treatment. I was ready to start my new life with a lot of lessons learned, my arrogance burned to ashes and my newfound humility.

Why couldn't I write about it then? As Rony had rightly said, I could write. I had decided I *should* write, so I will write. I opened my laptop and started typing. I started typing about how proud and confident I was of my body and work. When I was in the police academy, doing my MCTP, my friend, Georgy, told me once how one of his friends had been diagnosed with cancer. He had no bad habits, viz. drinking or smoking, and yet he had got cancer. That day, I had arrogantly made light of the news and told Georgy, 'See bro, he had no bad habits and he got cancer. One should have a bad habit. At least drinking. Drinking alcohol probably makes you immune to cancer.'

It is a fact that cancer has no proper cause. There is no definitive study concluding that if we follow some particular way of life, we can keep away from cancer. In strict medical terms, everyone has an equal probability of getting cancer. There are multifarious factors, the majority of which we humans have no control over. If you say this food habit is the cause, stress is the cause, or any other reason is the cause, there can be counter-theories with umpteen examples that can prove your theory wrong.

As soon as someone gets diagnosed with cancer, the first thing everyone around him does is scramble to find the cause. The situation is further worsened by concerned friends and relatives attributing it to reasons based entirely on hearsay and personal opinion, thus placing the blame for the disease on the patient, who is already depressed by their diagnosis.

I started typing away furiously on my laptop. The second wave of the pandemic was easing and people had started getting vaccinated. After months of lockdown, the government started allowing people more freedom of movement. My sister-in-law's marriage had been postponed twice because of the pandemic, and now she had finally got permission to have her ceremony with only twenty people present. Since I was unwell, I couldn't go. Remya and the children went, while I attended the function remotely, as it was telecast live. They were away for a week. I spent the days studying Arabic.

Even more people came to know about my cancer and started calling me, including my distant relatives. Those who called me unaware that I had cancer, I would boldly convey the news to.

After a week, when Remya and the kids were supposed to come back, she called and told me that they had all tested positive for Covid-19. Ishaan had a high fever. Fortunately, everyone in my in-laws' house had been vaccinated. Remya had got only one dose and had a harder time than the others. However, God was kind enough to ensure that their infection was detected the day they were planning to come back to our home. If it had been delayed, my life would have been in grave danger.

Two more weeks of isolation and loneliness followed. It was good that I had Arabic to keep occupied, or I would surely have sought out treatment for depression. Studying helped keep my sanity intact during this time. I had been learning the language for almost three months. Now I could easily write it, and could even read and speak a little.

There were still two more weeks before my scan. Remya was fighting against Covid-19, racked by tremendous body aches, headaches and tiredness. Fortunately, the kids were doing better, but at some point, Ishaan had fallen off his bed and suffered a head injury. He needed stitches on the back of his head. 'Cancer, chickenpox, Covid-19, low-immunity infection, head injury – are there any more tests we have to pass?' I wondered.

I started developing weakness and tiredness two weeks before the scan was due. There were ulcers in my mouth, and the right side of my face started swelling up. I developed a fever as well. I felt so tired that I couldn't sit long enough to study. Again, I found myself returning to bed. 'What's the matter now?' I thought. Since I had a fever, I decided to go to the hospital. With Remya and the kids not there, I went with my mom. Fortunately, one of the doctors was there and did a blood test for me. My immunity was low, but not bad. They decided to admit me to the hospital and do a Covid-19 test. It came out negative.

Who was going to stay with me at the hospital as my attendant now? Not my elderly parents. I was supposed to take care of them at this age, and here they were, taking care of me. I felt miserable. The doctor attending to us was, fortunately, Benz's friend's wife. I knew her, so I requested to talk to her in private.

I told her that my family was down with Covid-19 and there was nobody who could stay with me at the hospital while I was admitted. I asked her what I should do. She said my fever was still low, which meant I did not need to panic. The only thing they were going to do was administer an antibiotic and an immunity injection. 'The peg!' I exclaimed. 'Can we avoid it, please? It is torture, doc. I can't bear that pain.'

She told me I had to and advised me to take a paracetamol to help bear the pain. I told her my house was a stone's throw away and if there was an emergency, I would rush to the hospital immediately. I begged her not to admit me. She was hesitant initially but then relented. She checked my mouth ulcer and suggested I consult an ear, nose and throat doctor (ENT) as well. The ENT said the issue was with my teeth and referred me to a dentist.

My brother's friend, Dr Sunit, worked as a dentist near our home; his wife was a dentist, too. My face was swollen on the right side, and the ulcers were very painful. So I decided to go and consult him, wearing a cap on my head and a mask. When he saw me, he asked if I was on leave from work. Since I didn't feel any hesitation in saying that I was fighting cancer, I told him of my condition. Though he was shocked, being a doctor, he reassured me that it would all be okay. He examined my mouth and said that one of my wisdom teeth was the culprit. It had been infected. For a normal person, this wouldn't have been a problem, but because of the cancer and chemotherapy, my immunity was low, and so my gum near my wisdom tooth had inflamed due to a bacterial infection. He prescribed me medicine for a week.

I don't know why, but I was completely shattered by this new inconvenience. 'What is this, God? Don't you want me to come out of this ordeal? Why are you giving me more and more challenges?' I felt all alone in this world. I lost interest in Arabic as well. I don't know whether it was because I spent too much time on it and was bored, or because of the wisdom tooth infection, but I quit studying. I stopped writing as well. I just wanted my scan to be over and to get the hell out of this medical nightmare. I thought I would feel better only once I had left home and resumed work.

I think this is the case with all human beings. We are always unhappy in the present moment. We never enjoy it; we are always either thinking about the future, or the past. But the only thing that is available to us is the present moment. Though our body is in sync with what is happening around us, our minds are totally disconnected from the present moment, in my experience. The further we are from the present moment, the more difficult the moments are for us. People who have anxiety disorders are completely disconnected from the present moment, or in more technical terms, from reality. Slowly, I was also moving towards that.

The cancer, treatment, chemo, struggle and loneliness were getting to me. I lost interest in doing anything at all. I just wanted to sleep. My mind and body were both getting tired. No Arabic, nothing. I spent all day in bed. Time started feeling a lot longer. Anxiety about the impending scan also started taking over me. What if everything wasn't fine? What if cancer lingered? Would a bone marrow transplant be my next trial? Would I feel like Wolverine? The uncertainty continued to gnaw at me, my mind spiralling with unanswered questions.

# 11

Finally, the day arrived, and I went with my dad to get the PET scan done. In the waiting room, five of us, including myself, awaited our turn for the procedure. Among the group were three men and two women, with me being the youngest. Despite my nerves, I still remember each of them because of the emotional upheaval I underwent that day. My anxiety was so high, the people surrounding me only made me more anxious.

Two of them, a man and an old woman, had come for their PET scan to determine if they had cancer or not. I asked the man what had happened. He told me his entire body had swollen because of intense itching; before coming to MCC, he had roamed around looking for the right treatment. He had been to so many doctors, until finally someone suggested he gets checked out at MCC, and here he was. The other lady was completely silent. She just told me she had come for her first PET. She was quite old as well.

The second man, I still remember his name well: Khalid. He was a retired Arabic teacher. The fact that I knew Arabic brought us very close very fast, and we started talking about a variety of things. He had undergone a full chemotherapy cycle like me, eighteen months ago, and had completely recovered. Recently, he had developed pain and shivering, much like the symptoms he had before he had been diagnosed. He was covered in a thick blanket and still shivering. For almost fifteen months, everything had been fine. He was afraid now that he was having a relapse.

The way he was shivering and from the description of his symptoms, I too assumed he had relapsed. The thought made me very anxious. What if I had a relapse? Arjun had described the ordeal he had undergone. Would I have to undergo the painful bone marrow transplant process and chemo again?

One by one, we were called inside. I went in. The radioactive substance was injected into my body and I lay under the scanner. I felt the warm liquid spread throughout the body once more. After the scan, I was given some tea, since I had been on an empty stomach. We waited for an hour and then we were allowed to go.

Just as my scan was done, the radiologist suddenly came looking for me. His name was Dr Nikhil – he was an old friend of Mohan and I. Our fathers were good friends. Recognizing my name, he came looking for me, asked after my health and we had a long chat about life. It was good that I had met Nikhil; now I could find out my PET results without delay. He said he would check and tell me in some time.

After a while, there was an announcement beckoning me for a scan again. Nikhil came and said that the chest part wasn't clear in the scan, so I would have to undergo a second scan for just the chest area. I asked him out of anxiety, 'Is everything fine? Why are you scanning me again?'

He said, 'Nothing, bro, it's because you might have moved when the chest area was being scanned, so we will need to do it once more.' I went again; my body went inside and outside of the PET machine.

After some time, I was told that I could go. I went and met Nikhil, and he said, 'Wait, I am checking the report.' I was anxious because when I had had my first PET scan, the radiologist had immediately given me a hint of what the report might say. 'Why is there a delay now? That too from a doctor I know personally. Why is he saying it would take time?' Nikhil said everything seemed okay. That brought me comfort. I reached home. Everyone was anxious. I told them about Nikhil, how we met and what he said. They were all happy.

But I was still waiting. I couldn't hold it in and texted Nikhil. He replied with, 'Don't worry, scan looks like a good response to chemotherapy. We need to discuss this with Chandran sir. I couldn't do it because it's Saturday. You will get an update on Monday.' He added, 'Relax, everything will be fine.'

I replied with, 'I don't want to go through this ordeal again.'

'I know things were rough. They will get better.'

I called Benz. He said he couldn't reach either Dr Nair or Dr Nikhil. Just had to get through Sunday now. Monday, I would have the report. Then I would return to Goa and to life – my life, my new life. Sunday morning, Benz called me and said, 'Let's go for a long drive.' I was happy to hear it. He told me to get ready by 11 a.m. and he would come and pick me up in his Benz. I was excited. I hadn't left the house in a long time. I was excited about going for a ride with Benz in his Benz!

At 11:30 a.m., Benz arrived. We drove around and headed to Wayanad. One of his cousins lived there. We had lunch there and then visited his cousin's oil factory. It was a wonderful setup. We had a great time, laughing at stories from old times; how we were partners in crime and would share our visions, ambitions and ideas about the future with each other. After a long day out, we returned home. I felt rejuvenated; fresh and spirited.

We were about to reach home when Benz started talking again. He said he had had a word with Nikhil, who had said that although almost all my cancerous lymph nodes had disappeared, there was something on the left side of my chest. Some cancerous activity appeared to still be present. He had then talked to Dr Nair about it, who had said that it could be anything; to confirm whether it was cancer or not, I would have to undergo a biopsy again. Tomorrow, on Monday, Dr Nair was going to tell me all this directly. If it's found to be cancer, it would mean that chemo had failed and I would have to undergo a bone marrow transplant and a different chemotherapy regimen, as our common friend Arjun had. He said all these things in a single breath.

It took me a minute to understand what he was talking about. When I understood, I asked him, 'What did you say? Come again. What are you talking about?' He said the same things again. It took me some time to digest what he had said. 'Chemo has failed. Now I have to undergo a bone marrow transplant. I am now the Wolverine. They will remove my bone marrow and insert new bone marrow, and then again, they will make me undergo more chemo therapy. My life will become hell. My life is over. The future is bleak. There is no future. It is going to be a totally different world. Arjun still felt tremors and shocks after the entire treatment ...'

I was sad, angry and frustrated. 'I knew it. That's why Nikhil didn't tell me about the report. That's why he kept stalling me,' I told Benz. He said, 'Tomorrow you will meet Chandran sir and he will tell you all the details. Don't tell anyone till tomorrow because your family will be disappointed and shattered.' But I was already shattered. I was so angry that I wanted to abuse God. I asked Benz what was next. He said that if a biopsy confirmed cancer, a bone marrow transplant was next. It is both painful and expensive. Even at MCC, it would cost lakhs. In a private hospital, it would be costlier. I started getting dizzy. Benz asked me to calm down, go home and get some sleep. Dr Nair would tell me the details.

That entire night, I couldn't sleep. I cried all alone in my room. What would I do for the next one year? I was told that the additional treatment would take a year. What about money? The treatment is so expensive. Where will I manage the money? I have already emptied my pockets.

I had planned that I would join back and take leave again in advance for the next leg of medical treatment. My DGP and Chief Secretary had been very supportive throughout. I talked to Tariq Thomas, my good friend and my greatest supporter. He is the most intelligent and upright IAS officer I have ever met and has been my guide and friend since my posting in Lakshadweep. He was the first person with whom I had discussed work matters, when I was diagnosed. He told me he would find a way. But he told me wait and see what doctor had to say.

'What if the doctor doesn't allow me to go and join work? What if there was no proper treatment for this at MCC? Arjun had undergone treatment at CMC Vellore. What if I also get treated there? But where will I stay if I am undergoing treatment there?' I kept thinking, thinking and thinking. Eventually, I fell asleep.

Next day, we went to the doctor. Shikha was there to help us and told me not to worry, it was nothing, 'You have always been nice and kind. God will help you.' I went inside the doctor's office with a heavy heart.

Dr Nair started talking; I sensed that he was also a bit gloomy. He told me the same thing Benz had told me; that there was something left. Doctors were not sure what it was. There was a high possibility that it was cancer, or, he added, it could also just be dead tissue or some other infection. To confirm things, they had decided to conduct a biopsy of that bit of lung tissue on the rear of my chest. He prescribed me a CT-guided biopsy.

After meeting Dr Nair, I went to Dr Nikhil and got a copy of the PET scan report from him. He showed me the activity area in the lungs. He said only a biopsy could clarify what it was.

While we were discussing these things, Nikhil started talking about the other people who had undergone PET scans with me. He told me about a man who had swollen to twice his size and suffered from severe itching. When I asked about him in particular, Nikhil shared a different story from what the man had said. The man had come to MCC a year ago with symptoms indicating the initial stages of lymphoma. He had been advised to undergo a PET scan but was afraid and ran away, trying all sorts of non-scientific treatments from local quacks. Subsequently, he wandered around for a year before returning to MCC.

Most cancer patients pass through this phase. Cancer treatment is difficult. There are no shortcuts. Yet many people look for shortcuts, unable to accept the dire news. Often, unscientific advisors, well-wishers and relatives direct them to all kinds of shortcuts. Most patients give in and try these shortcuts, creating more harm than good. They lose precious time and finally return to doctors when they can no longer bear the pain. By then, the cancer has often advanced to its final stages. Cancer progresses exponentially. The initial growth from stage 1 to stage 2 is slow, sometimes taking up to a year. From stage 2 to stage 3, the growth is faster, and in further stages, even more so. By then, the extent of the spread is so great that a return is nearly impossible. It is very important that cancer is detected at the earliest possible stage and treated in a scientific manner by a qualified oncologist.

Another good news Nikhil mentioned was about the Arabic teacher I had met before my PET scan, Khalid. His scan was completely clear, and he was unnecessarily worrying. When I met him that day, the way he was shivering and covered up, I had wondered if he was suffering from a relapse. But there was no malignancy inside his body. The fear of relapse made him feel all the symptoms without any underlying disease.

My biopsy was scheduled for 27 July. I met Dr Nair and asked if I could join duty and return later for the biopsy and further treatment, but he sweetly denied. I was worried about my leave and the expenditure. If it was confirmed to be cancer, I would have to undergo a bone marrow transplant, which would need a lot of money. Thank God that until then, I was only using up leave I had accumulated due to my service so far; thanks to the Goa government, I was getting a salary. But my leave would be over soon, and once it was, what would happen next? I didn't see any way forward. I was depressed and felt dead inside. 'Instead of enduring all these pains, it would have been better if I had died of cancer,' I thought as I stayed alone in my room all day. My mom came to my room occasionally, trying to console me. Because of the mandatory quarantine after recovering from Covid-19, Remya and the kids were still at her parents' home.

I was sleeping in the afternoon on the day before the biopsy. I had stopped my classes and quit studying Arabic. I was doing nothing other than sitting preoccupied with my obsessive depressive thoughts. Sleeping at night was very difficult, and because I didn't, I dozed off during the day. I had a dream that day. I saw myself undergoing a bone marrow transplant. I was in a hospital; a lot of tubes and needles were sticking out of me. I looked skinny and emaciated. I could hardly walk. When I wanted to go to the bathroom, I needed support to get up, and I saw myself falling over when I tried to walk. I suddenly woke up sweating. 'I don't want this. I don't want this to happen. God, no, I don't want this to happen.' I prayed hard. The entire day and night, I prayed, 'God save me from this ordeal, save me.' I prayed and prayed. I didn't spend one moment in silence; I kept praying.

My dad accompanied me to MCC, the next day. We waited outside the scanning centre. We had brought a bottle of water along, as instructed by the doctors. When my turn came, they took the bottle and then gave it back to me. It was now filled with chemicals to bring out the contrast in the CT scan. After drinking it, I had to wait for some time. All this time, I kept praying. The Bible says 'If you have faith as small as a mustard seed, you can say to this mountain, "Move from here to there", and it will move. Nothing will be impossible for you.' Such is the power of belief. I went on praying, my belief strong.

Suddenly, they called me: 'Nidhin?' I went inside. Along with me, my dad was called in, too. Though it was a laparoscopic surgery, there were still chances of the procedure going wrong. They told me that I would have to lay still on my stomach and then through my back, a needle would be pierced into my body. It would be directed to move towards the suspicious tissue, guided by a CT scan. It was very important for me to stand still. They would use anaesthesia, but there would be chances of pain. Once the needle reached the tissue, it would suck in a part of the tissue or fluid, which would then undergo histopathological investigation to ascertain whether or not it was cancerous.

Dr Nikhil also came inside to try to instil confidence in me. They took my father and my signatures on a consent form. After this, they inserted the needles into the veins in my hand and injected some chemicals. Then they changed my clothes and took me to the procedure room.

The CT machine, which now seemed less unfamiliar, was waiting there for me. They gave me one more direction: lie still and follow all the instructions that they relay through the speakers.

I was asked to lie down on the bed in the machine, on my stomach. I was praying hard. 'No more cancer, no more needles, no more chemo, no more pains.' I could feel tears flowing down my nose and onto the bed. 'Now the needle will pierce through my back,' I prepared myself. They guided me inside the CT machine, which might be used to ascertain the position of malignant tissue. I was still waiting for the needle to pierce me. But nothing happened. No instructions ... I was left waiting.

Suddenly, they asked me to get up. 'What happened?' I looked at them, intrigued. They told me that the activity area was too small. Doing a CT-guided biopsy would not work. If it was a malignancy, we had to give it more time to grow, after which the same procedure would be done again. I asked them what now, and the doctor came to me and told me that they would discuss it with Dr Nair and let me know. On the CT slip, they wrote 'CT scan today shows a decrease in the density of the left lower lobe. Only focal ground glass capacity is seen as persisting. Discussed with Dr Nikhil, biopsy is not feasible; shall do follow-up CT,' and the doctor signed under it.

It was a miracle. I thanked God a hundred times. As soon as I sat up, a big smile spread across my face. Seeing that smile, the doctor asked, 'Are you happy now? Let us wait and watch. The activity area inside the lungs is too small. The risk is not worth it anymore.' Dr Nikhil also came into the CT room. He asked too, 'Are you happy now? I had told you earlier itself.'

Then I asked, 'What about that dark spot? What is the future?'

He said, 'In cancer, there are always chances of relapse. There are many cases in which chemotherapy by itself doesn't work. In your case, your body has responded well to chemo. So now don't think about the dark spot and enjoy your life.'

I was very happy and asked him whether I could rejoin duty in Goa. He said I should be fine, but the decision was Dr Nair's. I called Shikha, who told me I could meet Dr Nair that afternoon. As soon as I reached home, I called up Benz, sent him what the doctor had written, and explained to him what had happened. He said it might just be dead tissue. He told me I get too anxious about everything, and I should work on; that I should immediately leave Kerala and rejoin duty. That is what I wanted. I just had to wait until the afternoon now.

I still continued praying, thanking God for the miracle. Around 3:30 p.m., my dad and I went to see Dr Nair. He also asked me whether I was happy, and I reiterated that I was very happy. I asked him about the dark spot, and he asked me not to think about it. 'Now it's over, whatever the dark spot may be, we will see later. Just forget that you had cancer and live a normal life. That's all.' We scheduled a check-up for November, after three months. Perhaps then we would know what the black spot is.

After two days, I again met the doctor and he gave me a fitness certificate. I decided to leave for Goa and join work within a week. The doctor had advised me to live a normal life. But with unfinished business inside my lung – a dark spot – and after almost ten months of relentless pain, ordeals, chemo and social isolation, it was not easy to return to a normal life; on the contrary, it was easier to be abnormal and deal with a difficult life.

Regardless, on 8 August, I rejoined duty.

# III
# Rehabilitation

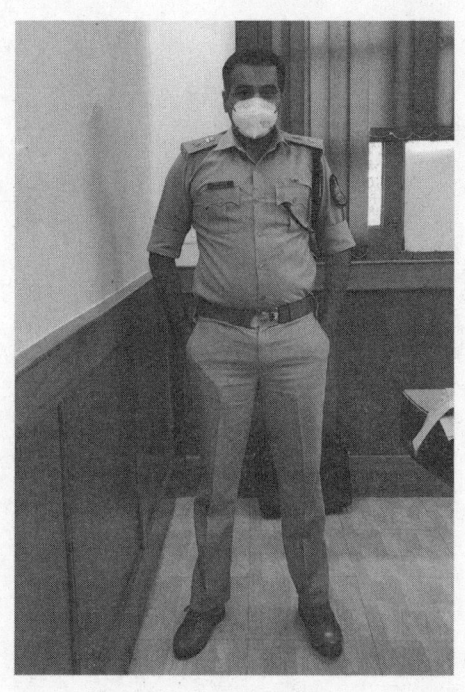

## 12

By the time I reached Goa, my official orders had come. I met DGP sir and told him about what had been found in my scan. He was totally cooperative and gave me a non-field posting. I called on IGP sir, the chief secretary and everyone else as well.

Goa was constantly lashed by rain every day. Back from a long break and after my battle with cancer, I noticed people looking at me with sympathy. I still remember when I met DIG Paramaditya sir. As soon as I went into his office, he got up from his chair and hugged me. 'Welcome back, my lion,' he said. Even SSP Pankaj sir gave me a hug. Most people were of the opinion that I looked fit and healthy.

My hair had started regrowing and my moustache was back, too. But I had got very fat, because of too much food, no workout and the steroids. To me, I looked like I had just got out of prison. But I was relieved to be back to work; it felt wonderful.

I was given an office at the police headquarters itself. My old staff started visiting me, asking after my treatment and health. It was really heart-warming to see people coming in to ask me how I was doing. I felt good. But the dark spot in my scan kept nagging at me in my mind. Restating over and over again to everyone, especially my seniors, 'There is something left behind in my lung that is abnormal; it could be a malignancy', the black spot became a permanent feature in my thoughts.

The spot was very clear in the PET report as well. The report showed a pre- and post-chemo scan of my body. Before chemo, the cancer had spread all over the body, except for the head and face in the top half, and under the knees in the bottom. It could be identified by its black colour. 50 per cent of my body appeared black before chemo. Neck, shoulder, lungs, stomach, groin, thighs – everything was cloaked in the darkness. In fact, the cancer was diagnosed so late that it had penetrated deep into my stomach, kidneys, lungs and even bone marrow. My body had responded well to chemotherapy, and the post-chemo picture showed that the dark spots had completely disappeared. My body appeared much healthier and cleaner, too, with the exception of one small dark spot remaining on the left side of my chest, just beneath the lungs.

When the pandemic was at its peak, I received my first vaccine shot following chemotherapy, but I still needed the second dose to ensure complete protection.

I adopted stringent safety measures, wearing double masks whenever I was outside, sanitizing my hands frequently, and taking a shower immediately upon returning home. I limited my outings to the office and home, and used up at least one bottle of sanitiser a day. I was acutely aware that contracting Covid-19 could be extremely dangerous for me.

Another significant change was my diet, which now consisted exclusively of home-cooked meals. I followed the dietician's advice to reduce the consumption of red meat and shellfish, which limited my food options.

Before my cancer treatment had begun, I had reached my lowest weight at 72 kilograms. However, after the treatment, the combination of heavy steroids and dietary changes had caused me to gain a considerable amount of weight, surpassing 90 kilograms, and leading to a noticeable increase in my waistline. My daughter Niya even joked if I was carrying a baby inside my stomach.

Fortunately, my bosses at work were understanding of my recent battle with cancer and ensured that I didn't have to take on outdoor duties that might be physically demanding. The DGP I was working under was particularly considerate and allowed me to stick to my daily routine. My doctor had advised maintaining a stable routine, emphasizing proper sleep, hydration and a balanced diet.

My mornings typically began at around 6 a.m. with a short walk in the nearby Jogger's Park; I carried sanitizer to these walks, too. The park served as a reminder of the days when I was grappling with the initial symptoms of cancer. I had attempted to do push-ups at specific spots in the park then, but I was limited by severe knee and wrist pain. My endurance was still limited, and I could only manage to walk for about twenty minutes.

Once I arrived at the office, my workload was substantial, involving dealing with various headquarters matters. Staying hydrated and frequently sanitizing my hands became routine as I dealt with numerous files every day. Gradually, I began adjusting to this new phase of life. I continued my morning walks with double masks and felt increasingly comfortable. My weight, however, continued to rise, crossing 95 kilograms and resulting in a prominent belly.

After two weeks, additional responsibilities were placed upon me, causing files to accumulate in my office. The increased workload led to moments of agitation. Whether it was due to the after-effects of chemotherapy or the sudden increase in my work responsibilities, I started feeling a growing sense of frustration. I had expected more understanding from my workplace, considering my recent battle with cancer. My suppressed frustration seemed to resurface in the form of sudden bursts of anger. One evening, over a small argument with Remya, I even lost my temper in front of my children, hurling a teacup at the wall and hurling harsh words to give vent to my frustration.

I was disturbed by the incident and upon reflection, realized that the issue lay within me. The eight months of patience and endurance from my loved ones had conditioned my mind to expect the same treatment from everyone else in my surroundings as well. I needed to find a way to manage my emotions.

The solution, I determined, was to reintroduce yoga into my life. Yoga, which I had practised before my cancer diagnosis, seemed like a promising path to regain control over my emotions. I began attending classes again, with IGP sir joining me on alternate days. Through yoga and meditation, I started to regain my sense of well-being and my mental composure.

My seniors, including my DIGP, IGP, DGP and Chief Secretary, were aware of my recent struggles and continued to be supportive and understanding. The DGP, in particular, encouraged me to maintain my daily routine, and pace myself as I worked through the mounting responsibilities.

However, my concern about the dark spot in my lungs from the PET scan began to consume me. The fear of a relapse haunted me, causing me to frequently check my neck and underarm areas for any signs of lymph node swelling.

During the initial days of experiencing symptoms, I had suffered severe chest pain, and now, I would often feel phantom chest pain due to my knowledge of the disease and the fear of its return. My mind was fixated on the left side of my lungs, causing me to have recurring dreams and visions of a black spot deep within my chest, potentially growing back into cancer. The possibility of it being a different, more aggressive cancer – like lung cancer – also crossed my mind. I knew that such a diagnosis would require additional treatment.

Cancer occupied a significant portion of my mind, taking up almost a quarter of my mental space. Even mosquito bites had severe reactions on my body, causing large boils and great discomfort. By this time, I also began experiencing chest pain recurrently.

## 13

As my work routine settled into familiarity, my mind found itself wandering more frequently. Past memories and cancer-related anxieties resurfaced, casting a shadow over my peace of mind. Though I resumed my morning walks, they remained brief, unable to counteract the weight gain I grappled with. Recognizing the need to regain control over my thoughts, I returned to meditation – a practice set aside during my cancer diagnosis. Arabic language classes offered solace, engaging my mind in a comforting mental exercise. Additionally, I began practising meditation daily, reading about its principles and applying them to my daily routine. Meditation sessions became a part of my daily morning and evening rituals. Whenever I wasn't meditating, I devoted time to learning Arabic, spent quality time with my children and tutored them.

In the mornings, after my walks, I went to my yoga class at the police officers' mess. I'd sit behind

IGP Rajesh Kumar sir, and spend twenty to thirty minutes of the session meditating. I even undertook a hundred-day meditation challenge on YouTube, which involved focusing on a specific sound. Meditation became a valuable tool in my journey to regain control over my thoughts and emotions in the wake of my battle with cancer.

Practising meditation helped me find inner calm, but the persistent anxiety related to my cancer experience still managed to overwhelm me. I started experiencing recurring chest pains and developed a habit of waking up at night, anxiously checking for enlarged lymph nodes and lumps in my chest.

My increased weight also had a negative impact on my self-confidence. After nearly eight months of social isolation, I found it challenging to engage socially. Feelings of unwantedness began to creep into my mind. Due to prevalence of Covid-19 and my compromised immunity post chemotherapy, I had made the decision to distance myself from people.

Habits are hard to break and I had developed the habit of constant worry and anxiety. I wondered if I was experiencing post-traumatic stress disorder (PTSD) or if this was an after-effect of battling cancer and undergoing chemotherapy for nearly a year.

By September, almost a month after my return to Goa, my mind had taken complete control of me. Sleepless nights punctuated by chest pains – which I later discovered were caused by the pimples on my chest. Thankfully, my meditation practice helped me maintain some level of control, preventing a complete emotional breakdown. The uncertainty surrounding my health was incredibly distressing – was it cancer again, or just a benign condition?

I sought answers and began reaching out to doctors at MCC and friends with a medical background. Their advice was to wait, but I just couldn't bear the uncertainty any longer. I knew what I needed to do – stay calm, be patient and maintain a positive outlook. These were all simple in theory, but increasingly elusive for me.

To find a solution, I recalled that during my cancer treatment, regular blood tests were conducted to monitor my health. Changes in certain blood markers were effective early indicators of cancer. I decided to get a blood test done well before the scheduled November check-up, hoping it would provide insight into whether my cancer was returning or not.

But how could I arrange for a blood test? When I consulted with Benz, he became frustrated and scolded me for overthinking. He assured me that there was no cancer in my body and urged me to focus on my work. Though I was hesitant, my anxious mind sought answers.

I made an appointment with an oncologist at GMC, which turned out to be one of my hastiest and most ill-considered decisions. When I arrived at the clinic, the room was crowded with patients. Despite being double-masked and diligently sanitizing my hands, I couldn't endure the wait for too long and found a seat.

I requested the oncologist to prescribe the necessary blood tests and was very persistent and patient with my requests. She finally agreed and also suggested an ultrasound scan, which required me to remove my shirt. I managed to get the blood tests done.

The results were delivered in two days, and I met the doctor to discuss them. The results were perplexing, as some parameters showed abnormalities. The ultrasound indicated a fatty liver, likely a result of chemotherapy, and potentially reversible. However, the doctor refrained from providing a clear opinion on the presence of cancer. She suggested taking a monthly injection of Rituximab as part of R-CHOP to prevent a relapse. When I enquired whether this treatment would guarantee that the cancer didn't recur, she couldn't give me a definite answer. Taking this injection would increase hair loss and other side effects of chemotherapy. However, it would be a lifelong commitment. I found this suggestion to be too absurd and promptly declined it.

The idea of blood tests to assess whether the black spot near my lungs was cancer or not was also thus defeated. I was left in uncertainty. The chest pain became more frequent after the consultation as well.

Was the chest pain real or imaginary? This time, instead of doctors, I asked myself this question.

The entire plan had failed. So what now? Soon, things took a different turn. After four days of visiting GMC, I started having a cough and runny nose. The dry cough became persistent. By evening, I had developed a low-grade fever. The new pandemic wave had reduced in intensity by that time. Almost all Goans were vaccinated. However, I had taken only one vaccine. Only after my chemotherapy treatment could I take the vaccine. And since there was a cooling period between the first and second vaccine, I hadn't yet taken my second dose. But I felt certain that it could not be Covid. I had meticulously followed all the protocols.

Even so, considering my low immunity and precarious health, I went to the doctor in the evening in Panaji. The doctor suggested we check for dengue and typhoid, and since my immunity was low, we should also test for Covid. 'There is no chance I have it. It is an ordinary fever, a viral fever, that's all,' I told him confidently.

The doctor made arrangements for a rapid antigen test in his clinic. The swab was put in a small testing instrument, and if I was positive, darker lines were going to appear. To my utter surprise, the instrument showed a positive diagnosis. However, the antigen test was not conclusive. It had to be followed by a reverse transcription polymerase chain reaction (RTPCR) test for confirmation. I gave a swab for the RTPCR test and went home. The doctor gave me some medicines. At night, the fever soared. It touched 103°F. The cough was also getting more intense and stronger. I was sure now that I was Covid-19 positive after all!

The next day, I decided to go to hospital. I went to GMC. I explained my condition to the doctors. They advised me to get admitted. But given that it was Covid, no one was permitted to accompany me. There was a Covid specialty ward, a good room with a bathroom and a balcony overlooking the entrance of the hospital. I shifted there. Again, I was alone in the hospital. My fever was not reducing. The medicines were not working, it seemed; the most they brought my temperature down to was 102°F, and I remained under watch for one, two, then three days, and it went on. From the first day I was admitted, the nights were severely difficult. At night, my fever touched 103°F, sometimes even 104°F. It was an extremely difficult time, and two nurses used to stand by my side attending to me the whole night, sponging me, trying to bring down the fever. Because of the fever, I couldn't sleep. I was also having nightmares.

The days dragged on. The coughing would not stop. Being alone was nothing new for me anymore. However, every morning, I had visitors – doctors and nurses – who came to take my vitals and to give me my medication. The situation started getting worse day by day. The cough became harder and more frequent. Tiredness increased. My blood oxygen level slowly started coming down, too. I began feeling immense fatigue. My fever continued to hover around 102°F.

After the fourth day, a group of doctors came to me, including a senior doctor. They started talking to me casually, asking after my health, treatment and my family. All four days so far, I had been alone in my room, either sleeping or just lying down.

The senior doctor suddenly turned serious: 'Look, Mr Nidhin, you are in a very bad state right now. You are going through the first stage of Covid-19 infection. You are not fully vaccinated and chemotherapy and the cancer have destroyed your immune system. You will soon enter the next stage, in which your blood oxygen level may drop drastically. There are high chances that you will have to be on a ventilator.'

I was shaken. Again, the fear of death started taking over me. From November 2021 until then, it was the fourth time I had felt afraid of dying. Death loved me so much that it seemed fixated on me. One way or another, it wanted to take hold of me. Already, when this was happening, I had been enduring a 103–104°F fever continuously for the last four to five days, extreme fatigue and a frequent dry cough. I was all alone with thoughts of death. I imagined a tall, stout guy with a scythe, completely dressed in dark clothing with a hood covering his face, standing right in front of me, waiting. There was a cloud of darkness around him; the only light was the one in his eyes. He was extending his left hand towards me and saying, '*Vaa* ("come" in Malayalam)'.

'So, Mr Valsan,' the doctor's words startled me. 'It's a worrisome situation. We are not left with many options, but we can try a cocktail. Though we are not sure whether it will work, we can certainly try it. In fact, if you are ready to be a test subject for us, we can arrange for it immediately. You take your time and decide.'

They left me alone. I called Benz and then Dr Nair. They said that the cocktail seemed to be effective and suggested I go ahead with it. I called up Remya. She had no idea what to say and agreed it was best we went with what the doctors suggested.

My chest had started feeling very heavy because of the infection. The fever was not subsiding, either. The symptoms were such that I was surely moving towards the dangerous phase of the disease soon. The pandemic had already wreaked so much havoc in the world. So many people had died from the Delta virus. In fact, everyone had lost someone to the disease. I was sure that I would also become one of many. My body had already been through so much – cancer, chemotherapy, so many medicines, injections and severe pain. Why shouldn't I try the cocktail? I read about it. It was actually a Covid antibody cocktail – a combination of two antibodies that were supposed to prevent further infection. It stopped the virus from attaching itself to the body's cells.

It was evening, and I was very tired. I couldn't even get up from the hospital bed. The fever was causing a severe headache as well. I called the helpdesk and told them that I was ready for the cocktail. Within some time, the doctors and team were ready with the medicine.

The cocktail reminded me of chemo. It looked exactly like the pouch that was used during chemotherapy. A pouch filled with a colourless liquid. The administration of the fluid was also done in the same way as chemo: IV lines. In 2021, I would have been pricked by needles more than fifty times in the form of chemotherapy, blood tests and administering medicines.

The nurses injected the needle into my right hand. It took almost five minutes for them to find the vein, since chemotherapy had shrunk my veins. And the medicine started flowing in. It took close to an hour. I lay down, looking at the drops dripping slowly and moving through the tube, into my body. The fever, tiredness and boredom slowly wore me down, and I slept.

I suddenly woke up after almost an hour with the incredible feeling of my chest being cleansed. It was really unexplainable. The feeling in my chest – it felt like it was being filled with a sudden rush of divine light. My lungs felt clean and instantly filled with clean air, erasing the heaviness entirely.

I took a deep breath and I felt so good and refreshed. The heaviness just vanished; the tiredness was gone. After fifteen minutes, the nurses came to check my fever. It had come down to 101°F. Everything appeared normal – pure divine intervention! The cough also vanished after some time. I felt all right.

The doctors still kept me under watch. Every two to three hours, they would measure my parameters, and in the evening, I was finally discharged. I was asked to come after a week for another test. Fever had gone and my temperature was normal by then. Once again, I had survived but I was continuing to test positive. I remained in quarantine until the test came out negative, which took two weeks, though I was allowed to remain at home. I felt very good and normal.

I had spent the entire month of October on leave. Two and a half weeks later, I was at my Goa home in my room, doing nothing other than reading, watching Netflix and eating. My morning walks had also stopped. My weight kept increasing and I looked like I was into Sumo wrestling.

Though Covid had taken my mind off cancer for a short span, as soon as I was back home, the thoughts again started up and so did the chest pain. But since I had had Covid, now I could attribute the chest pain to that. I discussed this with my DGP and IGP. All of them believed the chest pain was likely caused by Covid. The date for my next check-up with Dr Nair was set for 1 November. My anxiety heightened, disturbing my sleep again. I decided to get my check-up done sooner, or the anxiety would eat away at me. I called Shikha and requested her to ask the doctor if I could come in for a check-up earlier, two to three days before it was due. She confirmed that I could. I immediately took leave and booked my flight from Goa to Kannur.

I boarded the flight, and from the moment we took off, all those memories of the past year started flooding in, like a flashback. The uncertain questions and answers started filling my mind. 'What if it's cancer? The bone marrow transplant ... chemo sessions again ... what does the future hold for me?' I started sweating profusely. The chest pain reached its peak. The flight was just an hour long, but to me, it felt like a year.

When I got off the flight, I was feeling dizzy; my head was spinning and I could hardly stand. My chest felt very heavy and painful. I felt like I was going to fall unconscious. Fortunately, I knew the police protocol officer at the airport. I called him up and told him of my discomfort. Immediately, he passed information on to the Central Industrial Security Force (CISF) officers. When I reached to collect my baggage, I was so disoriented, I could barely stand. I went and sat on a chair nearby and got a call from a CISF officer. He came and asked me if everything was okay. I said I needed a doctor, and he took me to a lounge nearby, supporting me on the walk there. Within minutes of waiting, a doctor and his assistant came running to me.

They checked my blood pressure and found it was high. They told me to calm down. They checked my blood sugar. It was normal. Then they asked if I had any medical condition. I readily unravelled my past before them, even telling them about the 'black spot' which was bothering me. The doctor said, 'Sir, this is stress. You had a minor panic attack.'

I got a call from Benz. Someone working at the airport was a friend of my mom's and had called her and informed her of the entire incident. She immediately called Benz, who knew I was stressed. He believed that I had no medical issues; it was all because of my unruly brain that I had suffered a panic attack. He talked to the doctor who had helped me; he relayed the information about my BP and all. I rested there for a while. My chest still felt heavy and now my heart was hurting. All my focus was on my chest. 'What is inside? What was that leftover?'

As soon as I reached my parents' home, I immediately rushed to MCC. I had already called Shikha, and she had got me an appointment with Dr Nair. As usual, the doctor was measured in his words and without much discussion, prescribed a PET scan. Thanks to Shikha, I got an appointment for the very next day.

That night was one of the most difficult nights of my life. Because of my anxiety, I couldn't sleep. I called Dr Nikhil and told him that I would be coming. He assured me that everything would go off well. I kept thinking of all the possibilities – cancer recurrence, bone marrow transplant, chemo – and before I knew it, I had slept off.

The day finally arrived.

## 14

My father, C. P. Valsan, is a very lucky man. What I mean is he seems to carry luck with him wherever he goes. It was for this reason that I named my children Ishaan Nidhin Valsan and Niyathi Nidhin Valsan, including his name in theirs, against the usual convention. I always insisted that anything with long-term future implications, I always wanted him to do. Rituals for the *vidyarambam* (start of education) and the *choroonu* (first feeding of rice to a baby) for both my kids were performed by my father. Though tradition dictated otherwise, I insisted on his involvement, convinced that his touch would bring prosperity. On the day of the PET scan, I asked him to accompany me. I wanted his hand to guide our fortunes as he made the necessary payments and signed off, letting me use his luck to gamble.

We first met Dr Nikhil, who could make out that I was very stressed. We had a friendly conversation. This time as well, there were five people waiting for the scan along with me. Except for me and another guy, the other three were old people, who were not in the mood to talk.

Once it was my turn, I went inside the PET scan equipment. The radioactive liquid flowed into my veins and spread to my whole body. The machine rotated over me while I was pushed into and pulled out of it. And then it was over. Only a few more hours now, before I would know what the future held for me. Would I remain Nidhin Valsan or would I become Wolverine?

I was asked to sit in the waiting room. After some time, the attendant came to me and told me that Dr Nikhil was calling me. I went with a heavy heart. Why was he calling me? What did he have to say? Was there some malignancy after all?

I entered the room but before I could even sit, he announced, 'Congratulations. Everything is clear. You are now a free man.'

I couldn't believe it. I asked again, 'What did you say? What about the dark spot under the lungs?'

'It's all gone. Come here, I will show you.'

He pulled up a chair near his seat. He showed me the scan and compared it to the old one. In the old scan under the lungs, there was visible activity. In the new scan, there was none of that – everything looked normal. 'You don't have any malignancy left in your body!' Nikhil explained. We hugged each other.

It was the best news I had heard in all of last year. I went outside and told my father. Immediately, we rushed home, where my mother was eagerly waiting for us. Upon hearing the news, she burst into tears, hugging me.

I called Remya and Rony, then gave everyone the good news. In the afternoon, I visited Dr Nair, who, after almost ten months, talked to me for a long time without any seriousness in his voice. The first thing I asked after he said I was clear, was 'Why me? Why did I get this disease? Is it because I ate a lot of non-vegetarian food? Or because I worked out a lot?'

'See, Nidhin, it's just written in the stars if you have to experience all these things. As a doctor, I would say there is no definite reason for cancer. If I claim that there is a reason for cancer, then there will be hundreds of arguments and scientific studies countering my theory. So as things stand, it just happens. It might be that some of our actions and habits, like tobacco chewing and smoking, can increase the odds, but inherently, everybody has a predisposition towards cancer. However, only in some of the human beings does the predisposition materialize into disease.'

'What next, doctor? What about my future? What should I do to avoid relapsing? Should I change my eating habits? Should I do relaxation exercises?' I had a lot of questions.

Dr Nair looked very calm, as though he encountered these questions on a daily basis. He said, 'Live a normal life. Just forget this phase of life. Live life like any other normal human being. Just try to live a disciplined life – that's all I'd add from my side'.

I was both shocked and surprised; I expected a lot more of 'You should do this; you shouldn't do that'. But there was nothing. This was totally unexpected!

However, I was happy. At least now, I was free from thoughts of bone marrow transplants and further chemotherapy. Though I knew it won't truly be normal, I could try to live a normal life. We met the dietician for further advice. She suggested quitting alcohol and red meat for at least the next two years. That was something I had already expected, and I decided to quit alcohol and red meat forever. She also suggested I eat more fruits, vegetables and protein-rich foods.

Immediately after this, I called up Benz and he invited us to his home. We went over with lots of gifts. We had a heavy lunch at his house, and I headed back to Goa.

My IGP and DGP were very happy at my result. However, I hinted that I might need some more time to adjust to normal life. I would find it difficult to attend to heavy duties and would like to maintain a daily schedule, which was not possible in law and order. They assured me they would consider it.

∼

Life started getting back to normal. I was settling into a routine and restarted walking. I was also slowly getting used to office work. However, as soon as I had started to settle down, I found another surprise waiting for me. My DGP was transferred. I was walking in Jogger's Park in Altinho, when he called me and asked about the status of a file. After that, I went home and, an hour later, my batchmate Abhishek called and told me this unexpected news. The DGP had been transferred to Delhi.

It was really shocking for me. He was the one person who had witnessed all my ordeals. He knew me, understood my way of working, my life pattern, everything. He had always been very nice and cooperative. However, a new officer had been posted in his place, and it would take some time for the whole police force including me to adjust to the change. Furthermore, no one could truly comprehend my situation unless they had witnessed it themselves or experienced a similar ordeal in their own life. I felt very disheartened and decided to call sir. As always, he was in good spirits and advised me to embrace the unexpected changes in life.

Thus, DGP sir departed and a new chief took his place. My posting didn't change, but my duties did. It was election time, and I was assigned to law-and-order duties. I tried to maintain my daily routine of walking, working and eating on time, but sleep became elusive. About four days passed and I woke up around 2 or 3 a.m., plagued by nightmares and cancer-time flashbacks. Once I woke up at that hour, getting back to sleep became a challenge.

My weight had exceeded 95 kilograms by this point. I had noticed my stomach size reducing due to regular walks. However, the demands of law-and-order arrangements majorly disrupted my daily routine. Nevertheless, I continued with my Arabic classes, which brought me contentment and joy. I woke up early each morning to study Arabic before heading out for a walk.

2021 passed and 2022 began. The previous year had been filled with health issues for me. On 1 January 2022, I visited the Maruti temple and prayed for a better new year. However, fate had different plans in store for me.

In January, a new variant of Covid-19, known as Omicron, began spreading, and I wasn't spared either. I developed a fever and a headache, and testing confirmed it was Covid-19, once again. This time, I was better prepared, having received two vaccine doses and improved immunity. I went to GMC again, the same hospital where I had been treated during my first encounter with the disease. The doctors there advised me to complete rest and quarantine, confining me to my room for an additional ten days without office.

This time, the virus seemed less potent, or perhaps my improved immunity played a role, but I experienced significant fatigue. I spent most of the day sleeping and found myself feeling constantly tired. Eating and sleeping became my primary activities, and resisting sleep was a struggle. After four days, the exhaustion started to dissipate, but I still had seven days of quarantine left. Upon completing them, I returned to the office, only to find that I had gained so much weight that I no longer fit into my uniform. On Republic Day, police officers were required to wear a cross-belt and a scarf, and I needed assistance from a staff member to fasten my belt due to the considerable weight gain. It took nearly five minutes to get the belt properly secure. In the evening, there was a function at Raj Bhawan, the official residence of the governor of Goa, and one of my fellow officers remarked at my tummy, saying, 'You don't look like an IPS officer anymore!'

My running T-shirts revealed a pronounced bulge in my stomach, and when I took my kids to the park, I felt as though everyone was mocking my appearance. It significantly affected my self-esteem, and I knew I had to take action to shed the extra weight. Dieting wasn't an appealing option to me, so I contemplated taking up running, gradually. However, I had concerns about its impact on my knees, given the potential strain and the possibility of ligament tears at my age. I was in a dilemma about what to do but decided to start with daily walks and eventually incorporate running into them, along with yoga.

I shifted my meditation practice to my yoga sessions, replacing *yogasanas* with meditation. When others were performing yoga, I would sit on a mat at the back, listening to meditation audio through my headphones. I devoted up to forty minutes to meditation and also ensured I meditated before bedtime.

In the office, I began interacting with people more frequently, having overcome my initial fear of contracting Covid-19. It was no longer a concern for me. During one of these interactions, one of my inspectors, Satish, came to see me. He had recently been posted under my command and we discussed my health and weight issues. During our conversation, I mentioned my desire to prepare for a marathon and asked him if there were any marathons happening in Goa. To my surprise, he suggested I consider participating in the Ironman triathlon event instead. Ironman! What is that?

I was intrigued by the name of the event itself: Ironman. The only Ironman I knew was the comic-hero from the movies. Satish explained that it was a triathlon consisting of a 1.9-kilometre swim, 90-kilometre bicycle ride and, finally, a 21.1-kilometre run. Interesting! Completing a marathon was impressive but finishing an Ironman event and earning the title sounded even more appealing. I could say, 'I am Ironman.' I had some background in the three sports of the Ironman: running, cycling and swimming. I had swum non-stop for 6 kilometres during my posting in the islands, and I had also completed three half marathons (21.1 kilometres) and a 60-kilometre cycling event at the National Police Academy. So while these events were not entirely new to me, the idea of combining them in a single race was novel.

Neil, the Ironman coach Satish introduced me to, visited me a few days later. My friend in the US had recently sent me a Garmin watch, one of most reliable fitness-focused smartwatches. Though the watch looked less than average to me initially, once I met Neil, I understood it was sent by God through his angel. That watch would be my training companion for the next ten months. He took the watch from me, made some adjustments, installed the Yoska app – which offers personalized training programmes for endurance fitness users – on my phone and provided me with a training schedule. Neil had successfully completed Ironman events numerous times and now worked as the deputy director and head coach at Yoska, a start-up founded by Deepak Raj, who had completed the Ironman triathlon twenty-eight times. Neil assured me that I could complete the Ironman race and that I should focus on the training rather than the outcome.

He explained that the event started with swimming, followed by cycling and then running. This order surprised me, but Neil reassured me that I could learn to excel in each discipline with enough training. Despite my initial reservations, with the guidance of Neil and the Yoska app I started to feel more determined and began my Ironman journey.

# IV

# Ironman

# 15

The first day of training was focused on running. The plan was to run for one minute and then take a two-minute walk and repeat this for forty minutes. I decided to carry out this routine at Jogger's Park Altinho, which was nearby. Initially, I found it difficult to stick to this run–walk pattern because I wanted to run continuously. I started running, but after just five minutes, I would be gasping for breath. I decided to persevere with the workout but encountered a significant issue when, after thirty minutes of keeping at it, my left shin began to hurt severely. Despite the pain, I managed to complete the workout, but messaged Neil to inform him of the issue. He suggested I purchase a foam roller, strictly adhere to the training guidelines, and incorporate stretching before and after the workout.

The next day involved swimming and a strength-training session. I had secured a membership at the Marriott Hotel in Panaji for swimming, as it had a small 18 metre pool. The swim session required me to swim 800 metres, along with instructions on swimming techniques. While I felt confident about swimming, I found it to be rather monotonous. After completing my swimming workout, I returned home for an HIIT exercise – a thirty-second workout followed by a thirty-second break, in total lasting twenty to twenty-five minutes.

Initially, the training alternated between running and swimming, with intermittent strength training. Running workouts were particularly challenging and my shin pain persisted. Breathing became difficult after thirty minutes of running, but I pushed through and completed the workouts.

My daily routine now consisted of training in the morning, followed by meditation and Arabic classes. By 9 a.m., I was engaged in Arabic class, and after my class finished at 9:45, I proceeded to the office. Since I worked at the police headquarters, my office hours ended by 8 p.m. After returning home, having dinner and preparing for bed, I usually slept off by 11 p.m.

To accommodate my morning running, I had to wake up around 4:45 a.m., start my running at 5:30 a.m., which allowed me to reach the yoga centre by 7 a.m. After yoga and meditation, I hurried off to my Arabic class. The early wake-up was a significant challenge, but a strong internal drive compelled me to stick to this schedule.

Neil suggested that I change my running route from Altinho to Miramar, as the road from Miramar to Dona Paula was straight and relatively flat, a suggestion that I found to be beneficial. I later discovered that this route was part of the actual Ironman track.

Balancing yoga, Ironman training, Arabic classes and meditation began to take a toll on me. Within two weeks, I started experiencing fatigue, which raised concerns within me. Fatigue is one of the most common symptoms of cancer, but my routine medical check-up had provided some comfort. Cancer survivors must live disciplined, stress-free lives and get regular check-ups done to check for relapse. For the first two years after treatment, I had to go for medical check-ups every three months. My January check-up had seen only positive results.

When I consulted Neil about my fatigue, he reviewed my routine. He noted that I was overextending myself, especially considering my medical history. He advised me to remove some activities from my schedule. Since I was reluctant to discontinue Arabic classes, I decided to take a break from yoga but continued doing my meditation at the yoga centre.

The days with swimming workouts were more comfortable for me because I swam in the evenings, after completing my office work. I would swim for almost forty-five minutes in the Marriott pool. Strength workouts were typically done in the mornings.

As time passed, the intensity of the workouts, particularly running, increased. The walking intervals reduced and the running intervals expanded. During moments of fatigue, I would motivate myself with the phrase, 'Focus, commitment, sheer will', inspired by a quote from the movie *John Wick*. My playlist of motivational songs also played a vital role in keeping me going, and I managed to complete the prescribed workouts.

Once my overall fitness improved, I began to relish my workouts. Each night, before going to sleep, my mind would focus on the workout scheduled for the next day. The Yoska app became the most frequently visited app on my phone.

By March, I had shed 1.5 kilograms, and my running had become more consistent. I was no longer training merely to lose weight; my goal was to become an Ironman. However, I faced another challenge on this journey. I had initially believed that Ironman triathlon involved running, cycling and swimming in that order. I learned later that the sequence was reversed. While I was comfortable with swimming and running, the speed at which I swam was slow. In a conversation with Neil, I discovered that every Ironman event had a specific cut-off time, viz. swimming had a cut-off, similarly cycling and running too, and the total event had a cut-off of eight hours and thirty minutes. This realization was a shocker, as my swimming needed to be faster to meet the cut-off times.

Neil assured me that I could improve my swimming speed with consistent practice. I kept up with the swim workouts, but it became clear that I needed more help. At the pool, I observed some children who swam faster than I did, and it was evident that my swimming was not progressing.

Neil recommended that I seek coaching from a swimming expert, and he introduced me to Indrajeet, a renowned Ironman swimming coach who had trained numerous athletes for the event. I started training with him.

The coaching sessions with Indrajeet changed my swimming workouts to guided swims. As the intensity of the workouts increased, I could sense that Neil had become convinced of my determination to become an Ironman. I had shown him that passion and zeal alone were not enough; persistence, consistency and focus were also essential for success. My daily mantra remained 'Focus, commitment, sheer will'.

One day, he approached me and said, 'Sir, it's time to start cycling. We need a bike.' Neil took me to Probyke, a cycle shop in Panjim, owned by a man named Kunal. As I stepped into the shop, Neil pointed out the specific bike I needed for our Ironman journey – a road bike with distinct handlebars that curved like inverted goat horns. Riding a road bike requires a bent body posture for optimal performance. I questioned Neil's choice and asked him why we couldn't use a regular bike. His response was clear: only road bikes could provide the speed and comfort necessary for completing Ironman. A trial cycle was available in the shop and both Kunal and Neil encouraged me to give it a try.

Taking the cycle out, I realized that getting on it was a challenge. Riding was even more difficult, primarily because of the hard seat that left my buttocks in excruciating pain, not to mention the discomfort in my palms. Doubts started creeping in: 'Is this getting too tough? Can I really do this? I'm so slow!' After swimming, I had to ride for 90 kilometres on this road bike, when I was struggling to ride for even 100 metres right now.

Upon returning to the shop, Neil noticed my anxiety and assured me, 'Don't worry, we have ample time for training.' Unfortunately, there was no bicycle available at the shop that day, so I had to place an order and it would take some time for the bike to arrive. I discussed my goals and health challenges with Kunal and he was deeply impressed; unexpectedly, he gifted me an indoor cycle trainer. The entire equipment list was expensive, with the full setup costing close to a lakh rupees.

It was then that I realized the complexity of cycling. Each type of cycling, like every sport, had its own specialization. The right term for what I was using, wasn't 'cycle', but a 'bike'. Ironman cycling required a road bike equipped with specific features. We also needed to wear special gloves to reduce pain in the palms. To my surprise, one also needed to wear cycling shorts, which initially struck me as somewhat amusing. Neil informed me that no innerwear should be worn under these cycling shorts, which had built-in padding at the back to cushion the buttocks. The shorts also had shoulder straps, similar to a sleeveless undershirt, but instead of fitting around the hips, they rested above the stomach. I couldn't help but ask, 'How will I manage a bathroom break?' To my dismay, Neil revealed that during the Ironman event, participants couldn't stop to pee and would instead have to go in their cycling shorts. I found that quite disgusting, to be honest.

While waiting for my road bike to arrive, Kunal lent me a regular geared cycle to begin my training. From then cycling also became an integral part of my daily workout regimen. I donned my cycling shoes, a helmet and gloves, and set off on my bike. It felt relatively normal, but this was the first time ever that I was riding a bike with gears. On gear bikes, there are both front and back gears, with a minimum of nine gears in the back. Choosing the right gear combination for different terrains is crucial. Neil advised me to focus on getting comfortable with the bike initially; speed could be addressed later.

I began cycling between Miramar and the Dona Paula climb, using the gears that Kunal had set for me. I opted not to change the gears since it was not my bike, but my hands and back would often ache after these rides. Despite the discomfort, I felt a sense of accomplishment.

I would complete my strength workout, attend Arabic classes and head to the office right afterwards. I began experiencing fatigue in the late afternoons, which triggered anxiety. I reached out to Neil, who reminded me that I was not getting enough sleep and was pushing my body to its limits with my overwhelming schedule. Early morning meditation, training, Arabic classes and work had started taking a toll on me, too. I decided to cut down even further on certain activities to alleviate the strain. I decided to practice meditation only on Mondays, the day that Neil had designated as the rest day. Arabic classes were now on every alternate day – Monday, Wednesday and Friday.

Indrajeet's suggestion to start swimming in the sea initially gave me pause, but I eventually mustered the courage to try. Meanwhile, my new road bike had arrived. My first few rides were geared towards familiarizing myself with it. By this time, I had learned how to use the gear system on a regular geared cycle, and had also conquered the Dona Paula climb a couple of times. My speed remained under 20 km/hr, but the persistent back pain subsided, leaving me with just the occasional hand pain to worry about. Eager to achieve my goal, I was all the more excited now to explore new routes.

# 16

As my running and cycling abilities improved, my running workouts underwent a transformation. Instead of run–walk intervals, I transitioned to aerobic running, aiming to maintain a continuous pace for a set distance, often ranging from 5 to 7 kilometres. Cycling workouts, too, extended to beyond an hour, frequently lasting one hour fifteen minutes, or one hour thirty minutes. Saturdays were designated for challenging workouts, sometimes involving a 10-kilometre run or cycling for two to two and a half hours. While I could manage these workouts, my body would start to experience pain after two hours, affecting my legs, hands and sometimes, my back.

Neil emphasized the importance of not overexerting myself while running. He recommended maintaining a pace at which I could comfortably converse with a running partner, if I had one. This moderate pace ensured my heart rate remained within an acceptable range, and allowed me to complete the distance without exhaustion.

Regarding cycling, Neil acknowledged my progress but said that there was still room for improvement. He reassured me that we had sufficient time to work on it. I shared my concerns about fatigue after two hours of cycling. That's when Neil introduced hydration into my workouts.

It quickly became a vital aspect of my training regimen. He emphasized that keeping my body hydrated was essential not only during workouts, but throughout the day, especially during cycling. I was advised to sip water every half an hour. Neil pointed out the water-bottle holders on my bike and the importance of drinking water while cycling, without stopping. He stressed that during cycling, participants needed to remain hydrated constantly.

Neil introduced a dietary change as well that significantly impacted my energy levels. He recommended substituting carbohydrates with proteins, and I adapted my diet accordingly. According to Neil, an average healthy man should consume an amount of protein equivalent to their weight in grams, each day. For instance, if one's weight was 78 kilograms, they would need 78 grams of protein intake daily. Generally, our diets provide us with only a quarter of the required protein. I increased my protein intake by consuming more egg whites – four in the morning and four in the afternoon, shifting away from rice and chapati. This dietary change had a noticeable effect on my energy levels. Coupled with hydration, I felt more active and alert throughout the day, with no signs of tiredness or drowsiness.

My training and lifestyle adjustments, however, were still not showing the desired results. Additionally, increasing professional responsibilities had resulted in a heavier workload, as I was appointed SP Crime and given the challenging task of handling the SIT (Special Investigation Team) for land grabbing cases. The unpredictable work hours and interactions with the media and the public started to impact my training routine.

Waking up early became a real challenge. It messed up my whole routine, affecting my training, meals and hydration. On top of that, my training was getting more and more demanding. I was now pushing myself to run and cycle longer distances, followed by sea swimming at Indrajeet's insistence. He had stressed the importance of practising in the sea before the monsoons hit Goa in June, which would make it off-limits until September or October.

Swimming was my weak spot. Years of improper technique had left me with a lot to unlearn and relearn. Indrajeet often emphasized, 'Practice makes permanent', highlighting the importance of practising the right way to achieve perfection.

To complete an Ironman swim, I had to swim at speed of 100 metres in under three minutes. When I started, I was way off that pace, taking close to four minutes. It was frustrating because I aspired to be an Ironman, and that time wouldn't have cut it.

Running and cycling, on the other hand, I was more confident about. I had run half marathons three times and found cycling relatively easy to adapt to, even though I had started late. My cycling speed had improved, and I learned how to sip water during my rides as well.

One Saturday, Neil planned a long cycling route for me. He had confidence in my progress and reassured me, saying, 'You have plenty of time, don't worry'. But my confidence would soon be shaken.

Neil couldn't come and sent my colleague, Satish, instead. Satish was the one who had suggested Ironman to me. He himself was an Ironman and did the marathon in 2019. We embarked on a challenging route, which included steep climbs, and I struggled to keep up with Satish. He introduced me to cleats, specialized cycling shoes that attach to the pedals, offering better speed. I was in for a tough ride, and the steep climbs left my thighs burning. As we returned to Miramar, I faced a climb I had never noticed before, which was steeper and more challenging than the others. I was almost at a standstill, with my heart rate soaring. After that, the road became undulating, and my speed dropped considerably. Satish, who had been ahead, was now waiting for me. I hadn't adjusted my gears properly, and I was struggling.

When we reached Dona Paula, the descent was treacherous, and I was exhausted. Satish told me then that that was the cycling route for Ironman 2019. We had only completed one loop of the Ironman cycling track, and in the event there were three loops. Three loops! Doubts started creeping in. Could I really do this? Did I have the strength for it?

My doubts intensified when it came to swimming. I had improved slightly, but a 2-kilometre swim was on the horizon, and I wasn't sure if I could handle it. Saturday arrived, and a long-distance swim was in order.

Coach Indrajeet and his team set up two buoys in the sea for me to swim between. The goal was to swim 2 kilometres in forty-five minutes or complete ten loops, whichever came first. It was challenging, and I was nervous. The race began and I quickly lost my sense of direction. I couldn't see the buoys, and I struggled to stay on course. I tried to follow other swimmers, but lost them too. The sun made it difficult to sight the buoys when swimming back to shore.

I started to doubt myself as I swam aimlessly, sometimes following the kayaks or the sun, and other times adhering to the coach's instructions. I collided with another swimmer during the fourth lap, but I kept going. As the whistle signalled the end of the swim, I struggled to make it back to shore, realizing that I had fallen behind most of the others.

I felt defeated, wondering if I even had what it took to become an Ironman. I reached out to Neil for support and his reassuring words reminded me not to give up. Despite my struggles, I had come a long way from the days of my cancer battle, and it was essential to stay committed to my goal.

The road to becoming an Ironman was challenging, and I had my doubts, but I was determined to push forward.

I checked my Garmin watch, which showed that I had swum 1,232 metres at an average pace of 3.3 minutes per 100 metres. In the Ironman, the total time allowed was seventy minutes for the swim, and I had twenty-five more minutes to go. However, fatigue was setting in, and I estimated that while I might be able to swim an additional 500 metres in the next twenty-five minutes, it still wouldn't be enough to qualify – and I was far from achieving that goal. Sighting (seeing) in the sea was proving to be extremely challenging, and my Garmin watch revealed that I was swimming in a zigzag pattern.

I bumped into Satish during after swim and expressed my desire to speak with the coach. He took me to Indrajeet and inquired about my progress and where I needed to focus. The coach reassured me, saying, 'You are doing well. Relax. It's my job to help you qualify in the Ironman, and you will do it within forty-five minutes.' I couldn't help but wonder, 'What is this guy saying? Qualify in forty-five minutes? Even finishing within the full time limit will be a miracle.'

The monsoon was fast approaching, marking the end of the season for training in the sea. My cycling wasn't going very well either, and I was troubled by doubt. I considered abandoning my Ironman aspirations. The idea of going from battling cancer to becoming an Ironman within a year seemed nearly impossible. But in the end, I decided to press on and not give up. I had only gained from my training – I had lost weight, maintained discipline, avoided late-night parties and improved my overall well-being. Life had never been better since my battle with cancer had ended, and so I grew more determined to continue with my training.

I persisted with my training regimen, even when I went to my parents' home for my quarterly check-ups. Dr Nair assured me that there were no issues with heavy workouts as long as I ate well. I also stuck to my workouts while travelling, booking hotels with swimming pools and treadmills. I even swam a hundred laps in a small 10-metre pool once, during a trip to complete a 1-kilometre swimming workout.

I never skipped my workouts and they became increasingly challenging. I reached distances of over 50 kilometres in cycling and up to 12 kilometres in running. Neil introduced a brick workout of 35 kilometres of cycling, followed by a 2-kilometre run into my regimen. My hydration routine also changed to include lime water with salt for electrolytes.

I had to adapt to running in the rain, foregoing headphones for safety and abiding by Ironman rules. It was a significant change, as I had relied on music to push me through my workouts. My workout playlist was essential, filled with motivating songs in various languages. The beat of the music energized me, even when I couldn't understand the lyrics. However, I had to learn to train without music now.

The rain brought on a new set of challenges, but also made the runs more refreshing. To keep dry, I applied oil on my body before going running in the rain. My heavy workout days also became even more intense.

The universe seemed to be in favour of my Ironman journey, too – the Ironman Goa 2022 cycling route was changed. Neil explained the new route, which no longer included the challenging Dona Paula climb, making the ride more comfortable and less tiring. It involved a loop of 45 kilometres that I could complete twice to cover the 90 kilometres required for the race.

Training continued even as the rain poured, and I adjusted to running in wet conditions. Neil supplemented my workout with brick workouts to boost my confidence. I completed a 50-kilometre ride, followed by a 6-kilometre run, even though my legs were tired and I lacked the motivation fuelled by music. Neil's words of encouragement motivated me to keep going.

I held onto the belief that my journey from cancer to Ironman could inspire hope for others battling the disease as well. Here I was, diagnosed with stage-4 cancer in 2021 and declared cancer-free in November 2021 – just one year later – embarking on the path to becoming an Ironman.

# 17

Following the rainy season, my swimming regimen transitioned to the Goa International Centre in Dona Paula. Here the pool was relatively small, around 20 metres. Sea swimming was scheduled to resume after the monsoons. My workouts consisted of nearly 8 kilometres of running, an hour and thirty minutes of cycling, and swimming with my coach. Running was steady but at a comfortable pace, while cycling workouts shuffled between strength-building and endurance-building sessions.

Since the monsoons started, I thought I would train at home. I installed the trainer on my balcony and started working out on it. Doing strength-building training this way was interesting, but endurance training got very boring. Neil suggested I watch some Netflix series while riding. I bought a mobile holder and installed it on the handle. Watching episodes of *Narcos*, *Diriliş: Ertuğrul* and *Friends* on the trainer made the effort more interesting. All of monsoon this is how I trained. I didn't like it, but there was no other way. Immediately after cycling, I would take the car and go for swimming classes at the Goa International Centre. I had almost quit yoga since I no longer had the time. Except one day in a week, every day was workout day.

I continued with my Arabic classes. I couldn't stop them. On alternate days, I did my Arabic classes online with Fathima ma'am. Arabic was also quite taxing. There was a lot of memorization involved, and by the time I finished studying Arabic, I was exhausted. Then there was also work. SIT was very heavy work. There were late sittings as well, which affected my sleep.

Once, I caught a cold and developed a fever. Even with cold and fever, I wanted to do my workouts, but Neil strictly said no. He gave me a long lecture on recovery. It is just as important in training as working out. If we don't give our body time to recover, then it will affect the quality of our training in the long run. There are more chances of injuries.

When office ran late into the night, I slept late and still would try to wake up early and workout. But Neil insisted that my first priority should be getting enough rest, hydration and nutrition. Only then workout. If I slept late, he said I should not workout the next day. If I couldn't manage seven hours of sleep, I'd have to skip working out.

One day, Neil told me to try the Ironman cycle route. That was my Sunday workout – a long ride. One loop was going to be 45 kilometres. I was supposed to ride for three hours and thirty minutes. Finally, I was taking the real route.

I took my bicycle in my car to Miramar. I had filled two bottles with lemon water. Before starting, I had a banana. I prayed to God that it was a good ride. And then I started.

From Miramar to Casino Point, the road is very plain. After that, came the Patto Bridge, which is a slope. There, I had to lower the gears, both front and back, because the cycle would not move. Following the ascent, there was an equally steep descent. Immediately, I changed gears. Both front and back were now at higher gears because it is a causeway. I hadn't realised that the causeway was a deceptive track. My bike was moving fast like a bullet. A problem with the causeway is that there is wind as well. By the time I covered the causeway and returned, my legs had started getting tired. I would hardly have gone thirty minutes by this time.

Then I took the highway and crossed Merces Circle. Straight road and I kept sipping on water and riding merrily. Two medium slopes came; they were tough because the bike was not getting enough speed. Then there was a surprise – the Bambolim slope! My God, it was steep. While moving around in a car, I never noticed its incline. The bike was not moving at all. No other way but to lower both gears to the first. I kept pedalling. It was almost 400 metres. This was, in fact, tougher than Dona Paula. By the time I climbed and reached the top, I was exhausted and thirsty. I had to take a big gulp of water. 'It's okay. It is Ironman. It won't be easy. Let's ride some more.' It had started raining as well. Heavy rain. After the Bambolim climb was done, there came a downward slope. The bike was moving fast, and the raindrops were almost piercing into my body. I was drenched. Neil had advised me to always wear glasses to prevent insects and dust from clouding my vision, but in the rain, the glasses were even more helpful. They saved my vision from the big drops of water.

I slowed down. The rain was not stopping. But the ride was easy. After a slight upslope and a downward slope, I reached the Zuari Bridge, which was over the eponymous river. That was an easier descent; my bike started gaining speed due to gravity. But there were also cars on the highway, all moving very fast. I slowed down, just to be safe. Even so, it was difficult for me to control my bike. All through this stretch, I had to be careful about as there were chances of accidents. After that, it was a smooth ride until the Agaçaim under-construction flyover. That is where I had to take a U-turn. Riding there after having endured the Bambolim climb was fun, if not for the rain. My gloves and attire were soaked in water.

Riding a bicycle along the Ironman route is like going through life itself. There are ups, followed by downs. If there were downs, there were also ups. All the upward slopes became downward slopes, and all the downward slopes became upward slopes. As the Zuari slope followed this trend, the speed at which I had come down was lost as I began my climb upwards. The entire stretch after the U-turn until the church past Zuari Bridge, felt almost impossible. Climbing the bridge was very difficult, too. Almost ten minutes of slow and hard, laboured pedalling. The pedals were resisting heavily and my legs were getting tired. I kept sipping water. Despite feeling so much strain, I managed to climb over the bridge. But after the bridge stretch, there was yet another upward slope waiting. The rain was still pouring heavily. When I reached the church, I lost my grip and fell onto the road. The tyre skidded because of the slippery road underneath and I fell on my right side. By God's grace, there was little traffic so nothing serious happened. But my leg was now hurting very badly.

My wounds started bleeding. Thoughts flooded my mind. 'Damn Ironman. I don't want to do it. I don't want to hurt my body. I don't want to hurt my body anymore. One year, I have suffered all the pain in the world from the cancer and chemotherapy. Now I am free from disease. Why should I strain myself? Leave it.' My leg hurting, I got up, thinking I would ring for my car, put the bicycle in the car and return home. But as I stood up, I found myself facing the church. It was as if it was talking to me; someone was asking me, 'How many times have you fallen while learning to ride a bicycle? You met with an accident once on your bike. Did you stop cycling and riding bikes after that? No. This is the first time you are falling. You will fall again and again. True courage is when you fall, you waste no time in getting back up and moving again.' Was it Rocky Balboa, God Himself from inside the church, or just me talking to myself? I stood up, straightened the bicycle, sat on it and started riding in the rain again. After the church, the climbs got easier, and soon, I reached the Bambolim climb.

The challenging ascent before now made for a thrilling descent, and my bike gained momentum. However, controlling the bike on the downhill slope was tougher here than during the descent from the Zuari Bridge. I even lost balance a couple of times, but my familiarity with the bike prevented me from losing control. The downhill ride was manageable due to the increase in speed.

About 1 kilometre before reaching Merces Circle, which was located between the Mandovi River and the Bambolim neighborhood, the road flattened, making the ride smoother. It remained pleasant until Divja Circle, a junction with connecting roads to Ribandar,

Margao and Panaji district, except for a sharp bend that required me to slow down due to heavy traffic. After that, I headed back towards Miramar. Unfortunately, here, the former easy descent now stood before me as a steep uphill climb, presenting a significant challenge. I had to pause for a moment to take a sip of water. Both my water bottles were nearly empty. However, I was almost done with my route; I only had a few kilometres left to go. My legs were getting fatigued and I couldn't help but wonder if the distance had somehow increased, or if I was riding slowly, or if it was merely fatigue playing tricks on me.

Finally, I reached Miramar, which brought me immense relief. Nevertheless, the journey was not yet over. I still had approximately 5 kilometres to go, to Dona Paula and back. The final 2.5 kilometres to Dona Paula and back to Miramar posed a tough challenge, but I persevered. I had completed one loop of my Ironman training route!

But my workout was far from over. I needed to complete three hours and thirty minutes of training, and I was determined not to give up. No matter what, I had to finish. There was no running to do after the cycling, which provided some respite. I paused my watch, reminding myself, 'The more you sweat during peacetime, the less you bleed during war.' This was my training, and I had to give it my all. The Ironman event was fast approaching, and I needed to be strong and well-prepared. The outcome of the triathlon was not my concern at the moment; my focus was solely on training diligently.

Reluctant to tackle the Ironman route again, I decided to cycle back and forth between Miramar and Dona Paula. As time passed, I grew increasingly fatigued. I had just one more hour and fifteen minutes before my workout was complete, so I kept pushing forward. I managed to cycle for an extended distance, covering 60 kilometres, which was a significant achievement. Despite the exhaustion and the pain in my hands, palms, back and buttocks, I felt a sense of accomplishment. The Strava app, which analyses the workout using input from my Garmin watch, even congratulated me for achieving my longest ride. However, I couldn't help but feel some anxiety as well. I had covered only 60 kilometres; the Ironman consisted of 90 kilometres of cycling, followed by a 21-kilometer run. Additionally, there was a 1.9-kilometre swim in the sea. The 60 kilometres had left me almost entirely depleted of energy, and I began to wonder if I would ever be able to complete the full Ironman event.

I reached out to Neil for guidance, expressing my concerns. He reassured me yet again, saying there was no need to worry; there was still ample time. However, he emphasized the importance of building strength and recommended increasing my protein intake, suggesting adding red meat, such as pork and mutton. I was hesitant to do this, so I discussed it with Remya. She was unwilling to include red meat in my diet as well, given the advice of the dietician, even though my doctor had not raised any specific dietary concerns. We decided to increase the number of eggs instead, and I began consuming up to sixteen egg whites daily. Whenever I felt hungry, I ordered eggs and omelettes, much to the surprise of restaurant staff.

One day, I went to a restaurant for lunch with my friend Chetan. He ordered rice, roti and curries, while I looked for egg-based items. I asked the staff for eight eggs, which left them astonished. They were willing to provide only six eggs and informed me that they couldn't serve more.

On one of my official outstation trips, I continued with my swimming workouts and went for breakfast. Whenever I travelled, I made sure to stay in hotels with swimming pools, as I mentioned before. I also ran on the road in front of my hotel when I was on vacation and went to Gujarat with my parents. I refused to compromise on my workouts, except when I hadn't had sufficient sleep or was unwell. My dedication to training remained unwavering.

Training early in the morning came with its own challenges, one of which was dealing with street dogs. After 6 a.m., the dogs were generally calmer and sometimes even friendly. However, before sunrise, they could be quite aggressive. I had been attacked three times, once while running and twice while cycling. Fortunately, I managed to fend off the dogs each time. To protect myself, I had started carrying a stick while running and wearing a high-visibility jacket to avoid accidents. I also installed a blinker on my bicycle for safety.

Unexpectedly, I had to overcome yet another obstacle in my training, arising on the work front.

# 18

Around this time, I was assigned the responsibilities of District Superintendent of Police (SP) for almost three weeks in August. My friend Neil had warned me about the importance of August and September in my training; they were critical months. The workload and the round-the-clock availability demanded by the position of District SP could compromise my training and recovery. My new boss had assigned me charges of both the North and South Goa districts, which would be a lot of work. I initially planned to request my police boss to change this order. However, timely intervention in the form of my boss's friend, Varun, helped me avoid a major disaster. Varun told me that if the boss learned about my venture, he would ensure there were enough obstacles to prevent me from completing the race. He advised me to keep my goals secret from my boss and not to approach him.

As a divine angel, the secretary to the chief minister, Ajit Roy IAS, came to my rescue. He apprised the

Goa chief minister, Dr Pramod Sawant. The chief minister, after learning about my enthusiasm and effort, encouraged me. He recognized my journey and paid heed to my request to reassign the duty to someone else. My training resumed full-throttle.

My dietary concerns persisted, however, and I still lacked the necessary strength. My body struggled to keep up, likely due to the aftermath of battling cancer, enduring chemotherapy, steroids and Covid. I was determined to regain my strength and stamina, but my diet remained a challenge. Neil continued to stress the importance of nutrition, and I continued to get into disagreements with Remya, particularly regarding my desire to include red meat in my diet.

However, a conversation with my swimming coach, Indrajit, led to a breakthrough on this front. He revealed that he was a vegetarian and credited his strength and endurance to his diet. He consumed a variety of millets, including jowar, bajra and ragi. I was surprised. Ragi, or finger millet, was the key to his physical prowess. I was convinced this could be a game-changer for me, too. Upon sharing this revelation with Remya, we decided to incorporate ragi into my diet in the form of ragi malt. I started to feel a significant improvement in my strength and stamina.

Additionally, my training regimen evolved. My cycling workouts along the old Ironman route with

Satish helped me build strength. I continued cycling in the rain, and my body became more accustomed to cycling. Pain and fatigue became less of an issue.

My running workouts also transformed. I began incorporating runs in different heart rate zones, starting slow and alternating between fast and slow runs. I increased the distance, achieving milestones like completing a 21-kilometre run on a Saturday. Brick workouts involving cycling and running became more challenging, and completing them made my confidence soar.

My swimming skills improved as well, thanks to the personal coaching sessions with Indrajit. I began swimming with better form and style, even challenging and outperforming my fellow trainees. I remained cautious about swimming, as I had never swum at a pace faster than three minutes per 100 metres.

Despite the immense progress in my training, a setback occurred when a contagious disease – hand, foot and mouth disease – spread through the neighbourhood, affecting mainly children and sparing adults. Unfortunately, I was an exception and contracted the condition, which left me feeling fatigued and weak. This was a stark reminder that my immune system had still not recovered fully.

With continuous guidance and support from Neil, I resumed my training journey, making strides in both strength and endurance. The addition of ragi to my diet proved to be a pivotal moment in my training, helping me regain my strength. While there were challenges, setbacks, and a fair few surprising twists in my journey, my unwavering determination to become an Ironman persisted.

After recovering from hand, foot and mouth disease, Neil came to meet me one day and offered a word of caution. He stressed the importance of not compromising our training efforts. With only two and a half months remaining until the event, we couldn't afford to waste any time. To prepare me for the challenges that lay ahead, Neil designed two gruelling brick workouts for two consecutive Saturdays. The first one entailed a 75-kilometre bike ride followed by a 5-kilometre run, and the next, a daunting 90-kilometre bike ride.

I was fully prepared and enthusiastic to tackle these workouts. However, during the first brick session, while I was cycling, disaster struck as my bike tyre punctured at the 25-kilometre mark. I found myself near the police headquarters and decided to leave my bike there, compensating with a 10-kilometre run. A week later, I was geared up for the 90-kilometre ride, but at the 50-kilometre mark, my tyre punctured again, leaving me feeling frustrated and defeated. I discussed this with Neil, and he said that such mishaps could very well happen during the actual Ironman event. We needed to train ourselves in tyre tube replacement, carrying spare tubes and the tools to handle the situation efficiently. He even suggested practising changing the tubes in one or two rides to ensure we could handle it in under five minutes during the race.

As the second week of September rolled in, I diligently tackled my workouts, dealing with the various obstacles that presented themselves. During one of the brick workouts, which consisted of a 60-kilometre bike ride and an 8-kilometre run, my bike's handle got damaged just as I was about to finish the cycling stretch. This setback cost me over an hour, pushing me dangerously close to disqualification. Doubts once again started creeping in, and I questioned if I was cut out for Ironman at all.

My determination, however, pushed me to persist despite these challenges. But as fate would have it, when my kids recovered from hand, foot and mouth disease, my daughter Niya contracted conjunctivitis. I took extra precautions, but children can be relentless in seeking their parents' attention. Eventually, her condition did improve, but to my dismay, I started experiencing redness and itching in my left eye. This quickly escalated to redness and pain. At the peak of my training in September, I too developed conjunctivitis. At first, I thought it would subside in a few days, but a visit to the doctor revealed a more severe, highly infectious viral conjunctivitis, which was expected to take at least two weeks to heal completely. This news was devastating for me, especially with the race fast approaching.

Two weeks later, I visited the doctor again, and by then, Remya had also fallen victim to the same virulent disease. The pain in our eyes was excruciating, making sleep difficult at night and waking up in the morning a challenging ordeal. The doctor advised against swimming but allowed me to continue cycling and running with some precautions. Neil suggested using headbands to prevent sweat from entering my infected eye and advised against outdoor running and cycling.

However, my determination overruled the recommendations. I donned my glasses and a headband and continued running against all advice. I couldn't bear the thought of giving up so close to reaching my Ironman goal. One Saturday's brick workout involved two hours and forty-five minutes of cycling, followed by an 8-kilometre run in the rain, which I adapted to by cycling indoors. I went against Neil's advice, insisting on the extended training. In my quest to become an Ironman, I even ran on the treadmill, disregarding its potential impact on my knees.

I neglected to consider the structured and scientific approach in which I was trained by Neil. Swimming had always been my go-to for recovery, soothing my muscle aches and burnout after running and cycling. But after contracting conjunctivitis, I was prohibited from swimming and found myself engaging in high-intensity cycling and running all the time. I was pushing myself beyond limits, unaware of the consequences. The pain in my knees became unbearable, despite stretching.

The next day was for rest, during which I checked on my eyes but found no improvement. I checked with the doctor about swimming, who once again advised against it. Running and cycling were allowed.

But my eye pain worsened, and my knee pain continued. Despite the discomfort, I persisted with my workouts. Cycling remained manageable, but running became increasingly challenging. An activity I had always enjoyed became especially problematic after one fateful brick workout, which caused the pain in my left knee to intensify, just below the thigh.

My eye had still not recovered in the third week, and I had to do 35 kilometres of cycling followed by a 12-kilometre run. I was still not resting and was adamant about a heavy workout, even though my knees were hurting.

I cycled properly. After cycling, I wore my cap, glasses and a headband, and started running. I was worried about my knee. After 2.5 kilometres, the pain started increasing. It was a 12-kilometre run. By 8 kilometres, I was limping. Suddenly, from the opposite side, a car came and stopped right in front of me.

It was Neil. 'What happened? Why are you limping? Why did you run? How are your eyes?' he asked.

I said, 'I have developed knee pain. I was supposed to run 12 kilometres. I just did 8.' He said it was enough and told me to stop. I told him my eyes were getting better and that I should be able to swim after three to four days. I had a lot of questions. 'Neil, will I be able to do Ironman, bro? I have never done 90 kilometres of cycling. I haven't done 1.9 kilometres of swimming in the stipulated time. I have never done a brick workout of all three.'

He reassured me that there was nothing to worry about. We had trained enough to complete Ironman by now. If my swimming coach, Indrajeet, had assured me, then I needn't worry about swimming. He said I would be able to do the swimming bit within the stipulated time. He also told me that never before the main event do athletes get to do a full Ironman circuit. They get to do it only on the D-day. So, only after 13 November would I be able to truly say with confidence that I am an Ironman or that I have completed the Ironman race. No one trained like me, with so much discipline and consistency, he told me. He was very confident in me.

Then he asked about my knee. He checked it and told me it was IT (Iliotibial) band pain, and I needed to do foam rolling. Later, he sent me videos on how to use a foam roller. I didn't want to take any risks, so I kept doing foam rolling diligently. When I went to see the ophthalmologist for my conjunctivitis, I consulted an orthopaedic as well. He directed me to a physiotherapist.

There was no good news on the eye front. I was asked to wait for another week.

There were so many difficulties and bottlenecks in this last stretch. This was the third week I hadn't been able to go swimming. I still couldn't complete a 1.9-kilometre swim within the cut-off time. I still hadn't done 90 kilometres of cycling. I still always felt tired and found it difficult to run after cycling. Until a week ago, the one part of the event about which I was confident was running. And now, even that was proving to be so difficult for me. I now had IT band pain and severe knee pain to deal with. I felt more and more worried. On almost all my long bike rides, my bike had created trouble. Its tyres had got punctured or the handle had gone bust. What if something like that happened during the main event?

'What do I do, God? I want to be known as the fighter who defeated cancer and, within a year after that, became an Ironman.' To achieve this, I had been training since February. Never before in my life had I ever been so disciplined and consistent. I had never put in so much hard work for such a long period of time – nine long months. And now, when I was so close to the event, why were there so many impediments in my path? Was the universe no longer conspiring to help me find success? Had the cosmic divine force turned its back on me?

Around this time, one of Remya's friends, Sharmaji, a priest at Kalahasti Temple, called us. Two days ago, he had felt an inner voice telling him to convey a message to me. He wanted us to visit Gokarna in Karnataka, then do a pooja at the temples there. Remya made the arrangements for us to do so on the next Sunday.

On Thursday, when we went to the ophthalmologist again, the doctor finally gave me the go-ahead to resume swimming after almost three weeks. By that time, the monsoon was over, and swimming sessions in the sea had begun again. That Sunday, we had a long-distance swim scheduled, which I was really looking forward to.

Remya and I had an argument over this. She insisted on going to Gokarna, and I insisted on the swim. I didn't want to go on Sunday; I was ready to go for the pooja on any other day. Not on the day of the swim. I called Sharmaji myself and asked him whether we could change the dates. He clearly said no and added that the pooja had to be done that day at that particular time after visiting the temples. He said he would be coming all the way from Kalahasti to do the pooja for us; those were the instructions he had received while offering prayers to God.

Finally, half-heartedly, I agreed. I preferred swimming to doing a pooja, but I didn't seem to have a choice.

On Saturday, we all went to Gokarna and stayed there for a night. Ishaan and Niya were also with us. The next morning, we went to the temples. We prayed to Lord Shiva at Koditheertha Temple and took the blessings of Lord Ganesha at the Shree Maha Ganapati Deva Temple. To every god, I prayed, 'Make me an Ironman. I don't want anything else. Just make me an Ironman.'

What I expected was a pooja in the temple. However, Sharmaji had made arrangements for the pooja at a priest's house nearby. We entered the house. It was not a pooja at all, it was a *yagya*. All five brothers of the family joined in along with Sharmaji.

The priests did the rituals and the pooja, requesting all the gods to be pleased with me and give me their blessings. We had to offer rice, ghee and oil to the gods by pouring them into fire, at regular intervals. Sitting in front of the fire all through the pooja for more than four hours, was difficult. The main priest kept asking me to ask God to grant my wish, and my one and only wish was 'Ironman. God, make me an Ironman. Sun god, make me an Ironman. O Lord Shiva, make me an Ironman; Lord Varuna, make me an Ironman; Goddess Kali, make me an Ironman.' I don't even remember the names of all the gods we prayed to, but I asked them all for the same thing: 'Make me an ironman'.

After the yagya, I felt strong and blessed. When we got back, I told Remya it was a good choice. I felt confident and sure that any obstacles ahead would be taken care of. I believed the gods would help me reach Ironman.

## 19

As the event drew near, my swims got longer every day. Swimming had become my top priority now. Leading up to November 1st, our focus shifted to intensive workouts aimed at building endurance. Following this, a period of tapering off would allow for crucial rest and recovery, preparing us for Ironman. More and more people started joining the swimming sessions, many of whom had never swum in the sea before and wanted firsthand experience in time for the event.

I was happy to be back in the sea, but I was still slow. I didn't understand the problem. Most of the trainees I used to overtake in the pool were now overtaking me in the sea. Though my speed had improved overall, I was still the last and the slowest. I must've looked worried because Indrajeet noticed and said, 'Take my word for it – you will complete the Ironman swimming stretch in forty-five minutes.'

For my knee pain, I went to a physiotherapist near my home. He carefully examined me, diagnosed it as an M-band sprain, and asked me to ice it every day. The running workouts were intense, and cycling was focused on building strength. I learned to change tyre tubes and got my bike serviced. I also connected with a bike mechanic named Mehboob. Every day before I embarked on my ride, I got my bike examined by Mehboob. Once I started foam rolling and resumed swimming, the knee pain slowly started disappearing, though not entirely.

Another reason my knees felt better was due to an improvement in my cycling posture. Neil's friend and Ironman coach Agnel visited my home once and adjusted the seat and handle of my trainer according to my height and posture. He gave me tips on how to improve my cycling as well, such as pedalling with the front side of my foot, just behind my toes, to increase speed.

By the end of October, I had cycled the Ironman route so many times that I knew exactly where to increase speed, which gears to use, and more. What I had learned from the whole cycling training was to always keep in mind that I had to run 21 kilometres after cycling, so I needed to conserve energy and strength.

I was still not happy with my swimming progress. I had a friend, a swimming buddy named Gaurav, who worked as the General Manager at the Marriott Hotel. In the swimming pool, I used to overtake him, but in the sea, he was faster. One day, I asked Coach Indrajeet why this was. He replied, 'Why are you asking me? Try to catch him at sea. You will understand for yourself.'

Two days before the heavy Sunday workout, we had to swim 1.5 kilometres. I decided to catch Gaurav that day. I started swimming alongside him. I had trained so much that I could now easily see and breathe on both sides, swimming relaxed and in good form. Gaurav was swimming fast, and I tried to catch up with him. That was when I noticed that by the time I completed one stroke, he had done two; my cadence was low. I was stressing so much on relaxed swimming that I forgot about cadence.

There was another reason for this. I was always preoccupied with the fact that after swimming, I still had to do cycling and running, for which I needed to conserve my energy. But if I didn't qualify at all, I couldn't do cycling or running afterward, could I? There was no point in being relaxed; I had to swim fast. I increased my cadence, checking after every stroke whether Gaurav was beside me or not, ensuring I kept swimming at the same pace as him. Lo and behold, I did 1.5 kilometres in forty-five minutes. That was a real mood booster for me. Now I felt prepared. I knew what to do. I was ready for my

Sunday workout: my first-ever all-three-events brick workout. It comprised a forty-five-minute swim, 50 kilometres of cycling, and 18 kilometres of running. I knew if I managed to get through it, my confidence would be boosted significantly. However, I was also anxious. 'Will I be able to do it?'

Before the workout, Neil told me to come and meet him. He gave me half an hour of special guidance when we met. He told me, 'Sir, you have trained enough. You have trained so much that if the Ironman was tomorrow, you could do it. But Ironman is not only about training; it's also about the optimum utilization of energy, and supplying the body with the right supplements, electrolytes and hydration at the right time. Keep yourself hydrated; your body has to have a lot of water. Eat as much protein as you can. During the event, you have to follow a particular pattern of nutrition and hydration. Sleep early on Saturday night. Wake up by 4 a.m., and by 4:30 a.m., you should have a good but light, carbohydrate-rich breakfast. Then, before swimming, have a banana and drink water. After the swim, have one more banana and drink water. Every fifteen minutes thereafter, take a sip of either water or electrolytes. Once you reach 40 kilometres, take one energy gel. Never mix energy gel and electrolytes. Drink water instead after the gel. At 80 kilometres, take one more gel. Before starting to run again, drink water. Every 7 kilometres, have a gel. Keep drinking water and electrolytes at every aid station. Never forget this. Otherwise, your body will start cramping. All the best!'

To do all three events together, there is a tri-suit. For officers and government servants, there was a special suit with the 'Fit India, Azadi Ka Amrit Mahotsav' logo. The suit was similar to a cycling suit, except that it was one-piece. It stuck to the body tightly, and the padding on the buttocks was lighter than in cycling shorts. For the event, I had bought a whole new set of items. I got a Scott helmet for cycling, Saucony running shoes, a cap and sunglasses for both cycling and running.

On Sunday, I woke up at 4 a.m. and had lots of water. To prevent chafing, I applied oil all over my body. Then I immediately did my meditation. I imagined and thanked God for being able to complete the workout. I thanked God for making me an Ironman. By that time, Remya had made appams for breakfast. I had appams and a banana. Then I wore the tri-suit. I prepared six to eight bottles of water, filling half of them with electrolytes and the other half with water. Then I filled my back pocket with gels.

In the tri-suit, there are three pockets at the rear that you can reach into. One can keep their mobile phone in one (though in the event mobiles are not allowed) and energy resources and supplements. Gels are instant energy resources in gel or liquid form, that can be torn open between the teeth and sucked on. The only condition for their use is that they can't be coupled with electrolytes, and consuming too many of them can cause the stomach to feel queasy.

I checked my bike. The tyres were fine. I had put new tubes in both of them. Neil had also adjusted the seat. I loaded the bike in the car and made my way to Caranzalem. The swim began there. There were a lot of athletes present, many of them new to me.

I did my stretching, arranged everything in order in the car, and went for the briefing. The swim was only for forty-five minutes. There were two exits. One exit was after 700 metres, and another 700 metres ahead of that one. We were supposed to exit after the first 700 metres, run till the shore towards the first exit, and then run back into the sea, enter it, and complete the remaining 700 metre swim. After forty-five minutes, there would be a whistle for us to stop, exit towards the beach, get ready for cycling, take the bike and start cycling. We had to cycle for 45 kilometres, come back to the starting point, and then run 18 kilometres.

We were asked to stand in a row of six. I searched for Gaurav. I wanted to swim beside him. I stood in the same row as him. Our row was the fifth or sixth. Just like in Ironman, each row went into the sea at a gap of five seconds.

I prayed to God for confidence and strength. Before swimming, I had eaten a banana and drunk a lot of water. The goggles were new. To prevent fogging inside, I cupped a small amount of water in them before putting them on. The water wouldn't leave the goggles once they were firmly placed around my eyes. This method also indicates whether the goggles are water-tight.

The whistle blew, and we ran towards the sea. I walked into the waves for as long as possible. During training, I noticed that walking could be faster than swimming in the sea. So, I kept walking, my good height helping. When Gaurav started swimming, so did I, moving my hands very fast to match his pace. My cadence was high. After ten minutes, I felt my heartbeat rise. I kept looking around for Gaurav; he was still beside me. I started to feel a bit exhausted and imagined all the gods to whom I had offered ghee, rice and *theertha*, asking them for power. I swam, never letting Gaurav out of my sight. We did our first exit together and started swimming again. We swam together; I don't think he even knew we were swimming together. We did our second exit as well. Almost 1.5 kilometres completed. The whistle still hadn't blown, meaning forty-five minutes weren't over yet – I had done almost 1.5 kilometres in less than forty-five minutes! I went back into the sea, as did Gaurav. Now I think he was aware I was beside him. We swam, and when we had completed almost half of the second lap, the whistle blew. I could hear the whistle blowing repeatedly, so I stopped immediately. The instruction was to stop where it had been blown. I came out running and, when I hit the shore, changed the mode on my watch. It read: 1,522 metres in 46.23 minutes, at a pace of 3.03 minutes/100 meters. If I kept up this pace for 1.9 kilometres, I would qualify – not bad! Without thinking much, we ran to the beach.

I dried off with my towel, then had a big gulp of water and a banana. I filled my tri-suit pouches with gel, placed my bottles of electrolytes on my cycle, and put on my socks, shoes, helmet and gloves. Once on the bike, I started cycling very fast, imagining the ritualistic fire burning in front of me, as it had in Gokarna. The gods were happy with me and had blessed me. I could feel the strength coursing through my legs. I cycled fast, overtaking everyone who had gained on me in swimming. I never forgot what Neil told me: keep sipping electrolytes every fifteen minutes. I also cycled quickly on the causeway. The only place where I cycled slowly was the ascents. Within one hour and forty minutes, I had completed 45 kilometres of cycling, finishing two bottles of electrolytes and moving at almost 25 km/hr. I consumed one gel. My legs were strong even after completing the cycling. 'Oh God, thank you. Thank you, God, for taking me to Gokarna. *Har har Mahadev*. Thank you, Ganesha. Thank you, God.' I thanked all the gods.

I put my bike back in the car, removed my helmet and gloves, wore my running cap, and started running. I remembered what Neil had told me: run at an easy enough pace to keep up a conversation. After every 7 kilometres, I had a gel, and at every possible stop, I drank water. I had my headphones on and had finished 8 kilometres when, out of nowhere, Neil appeared beside me, cycling. He started cycling at my pace and talking to me. He checked my pace and my heartbeat, telling me to keep running at this pace. But he insisted I remove my headphones, which I was hesitant to do. He told me that in the real event, wearing headphones would mean immediate disqualification. I removed the headphones and gave them to him. Throughout my run, he cycled with me, kept talking and laughing. I didn't even feel like I was running 18 kilometres. He kept asking how I was feeling. I was okay until the 15-kilometre mark. After that, the tiredness started creeping into my legs and knees. Neil told me to stop. I had run the entire stretch except for the Dona Paula climb, which he had told me not to run. There was no need to run it.

When he told me to stop running, I said to him, 'focus, commitment and sheer will, Neil, I won't stop.' And I ran my 18 kilometres at a pace of 8 min/km, taking a total of two hours and twenty-four minutes. The entire workout was four hours and forty-six minutes long. I felt great, happy and confident. I told Neil, this was because of the yagya I had done in Gokarna that Sunday. Neil laughed and hugged me. 'Sir, you are going to be an Ironman.' I was still worried about swimming, though he advised me to not worry about it. I asked him what about the full Ironman brick workout. He told me we wouldn't do it. In fact, that day was one of the longest workouts we did. Now there would be one more long workout, after which the training routine – as far as cycling and running were concerned – would reduce in intensity. Even for swimming, the last week would just be relaxed swimming.

Almost all the people who swam that day had jellyfish stings, except Gaurav and me. I thanked the gods at Gokarna for clearing my path. That was 23 October, and three weeks were left. I tried to maintain my routine: sleeping by 9 p.m. and waking up by 4 a.m. I didn't go anywhere other than the office. I avoided group activities and wore masks, following all safety protocols for Covid-19. Now was not the time to get sick.

The next week, I underwent training to learn how to change the tyre tubes on my bike. Mehboob came to my apartment complex and trained me on how to remove the tubes, put in new ones, and fill them with air. Initially, it took almost twenty minutes to change a tube, but if there was one thing I had learned from the nine months of training, it was that commitment and practice are key. Repetition makes you faster and more efficient. Within five days, I could replace a tube in ten minutes. That Sunday was my next heavy workout: swimming, followed by 80 kilometres of cycling and 5 kilometres of running. I followed the same routine as the previous week, as advised by Neil.

This time as well, I looked for Gaurav and stood in the same row as him. This time, it was 1-kilometre loops with four exits. We swam 500 metres out, exited, re-entered and repeated the loop. We had seventy minutes. The swimming round started, and I stayed beside Gaurav. Our coach had given us enough training on how to exit and re-enter the sea, which was taxing, increased the heartbeat and broke the rhythm. Improper exits could cause cramps. Exit and entry training was also important because, after completing swimming, participants might have to run as long as 1 kilometre to reach the cycle stand. I did all my exits and entries properly. I couldn't catch Gaurav on the last lap, but when I finished my swim and checked my watch, I had completed my swim at a pace of 3 minutes/100 metres – an improvement. I would have just qualified or been just disqualified.

I ran to Indrajeet and asked how I did. He said again, 'Nidhin, take it from me. You will finish Ironman swimming in forty-five minutes.' I went for cycling and did the first loop properly. By the second loop, when I climbed the Bambolim climb, I started getting tired. I could cycle faster, but I had a run to complete after this. Training had taught me that the most important thing about cycling in Ironman was to avoid leg cramps. After the climb, I cycled slowly, kept hydrating, and ate gels as per Neil's instructions. I somehow managed the Zuari climb on my return. Just before the finish, I stopped riding and practiced changing my tubes. I had all the accessories and the full kit in the pouch under my seat. It took me ten minutes to change the tyre tubes successfully and independently. I finished my cycling: 83.5 kilometres in three hours, forty-five minutes. After that, I ran for 5 kilometres. By the end, I was tired, but that was all for the day. The total workout was six hours long.

Exactly one year ago, I was struggling to catch my breath, fighting cancer and Covid, and here I was, having completed the longest workout of my life. Close to six hours of swimming, cycling and running. I felt very happy and proud of myself. There is a song in my playlist from the Telugu movie *Chitralahari*. It goes as follows:

*Prayatname Modati Vijayanam*
*Prayatname, Mana Ayudham*
[Hard work (effort) is the first victory.
Effort is our weapon.]

I kept singing the song. I was happy. Even if I did not bag the Ironman title, I didn't have any regrets; I had trained to the best of my abilities. I had done my part. I hadn't missed a single day of training so far. While everyone partied and stayed up late at night, I slept and recovered; while everyone slept in the early morning, I woke up and trained. Never in my life had I felt so alive before. Never had I ever been fitter. When I started training for Ironman in February, I was more than 90 kilograms. Now I was at seventy-four. I had lost 16 kilograms in nine months, scientifically, without compromising on my nutrition. I had found a way of life. When I finished my workout that day, I asked Neil, 'What about after the Ironman, Neil?'

He answered, 'Sir, Ironman is not an event; it's a way of life. You follow this discipline throughout life.'

After that week, there were not many workouts – hard workouts. On 6 November, we did a brick workout. 1.8 kilometres swimming, 30 kilometres cycling and 10 kilometres running. Except for swimming, I managed both workouts easily. Swimming was still on the qualifying–not qualifying edge. Now, one more week was left. To avoid any last-minute official emergencies distracting me from my goal, I took leave till 15 November.

# 20

Goa was getting ready for Ironman. The Miramar circle was decorated with Ironman banners. All over Panaji, we could see a lot of new faces either cycling or running. I was also gearing up for the event. I kept doing meditation to calm myself, but it was still difficult. I was like a student who had been preparing the entire year for an exam, and the exam was finally around the corner.

The previous week, I hadn't done many workouts, except for swimming. On 9 November, there was a light brick workout with forty-five minutes of cycling and 4 kilometres of running. After running, I went for a swim. That week, we were advised to load up on carbohydrates and hydration. The entire Ironman crew was in Goa, including Yoska's CEO, Deepak, who had completed the Ironman twenty-eight times. Neil introduced me to the whole crew. Everyone was fascinated and inspired by my story. As a stage-4 cancer survivor, I had almost seen death. I had defeated it, and within a year, I could earn the title of Ironman. They all wished me luck. Neil introduced me with, 'Nidhin sir has been so committed, focused and disciplined. I have never trained a person who was so sincere, responsible and serious about training. He never missed a single workout.' All of them were rooting for me. I wanted the title badly. Sleeping and waking, I dreamt of being an Ironman. And within a year of beating cancer, I was on the brink of achieving it!

Finally, the D-Day arrived. The final day for which I had been working so hard, preparing so much. 13 November. The day was here. The D-Day. The day of the Ironman 70.3 Goa.

My leave for Ironman started on 8 November, until 15 November. In between, there were a lot of briefings from the organizers. There were briefings about rules, about cut-offs, and about negative marking if we litter the roads. I was only concerned about the swimming cut-off. It was seventy minutes. They explained the course for swimming, cycling and running. I was so eager about Ironman that I still remember being the first to collect my bib. I had reached by 8:30 a.m. The first person to get there. My number was 973. I attended all the briefings. Other than that, I didn't go anywhere. I sought an appointment with the chief minister, chief Secretary and IGP sir and sought their blessings. I went and met my colleague Ajit as well. I slept at the proper time and woke up at 4 a.m. But my anxiety was catching up to me. I was becoming more and more anxious. I paid particular attention to swimming workouts. The day before the event, I sought the blessings of Lord Hanuman at the nearby Maruti Temple. I sought the blessings of my parents – even though they had no idea what I was up to.

The previous week, I had a lot of carbohydrates in my diet. Other than that, I mainly ate eggs. In October, the number of egg whites I ate every day had increased to twenty per day. Eight in the morning, eight in the afternoon and four at night. Whenever I wanted to eat something, I had eggs or omelettes.

It was 12 November. I went to bed at 9 p.m. sharp, but I was so anxious that I found it difficult to sleep. Somehow, I managed to fall asleep, perhaps tired out by the anxiety. At 2:30 a.m., I woke up and couldn't go back to sleep. I kept tossing and turning until 3 a.m., unable to find rest. I was anxious, and due to that anxiety, I was ruining things for myself. A good night's sleep was crucial for optimal performance the next day, and yet, it eluded me. I got up and went to my study, where I did some meditation. I took out a piece of paper and wrote, 'Thank you, God, for making me an Ironman', ten times over. I did some more meditation. At around 4 a.m., I went back to bed and slept until 5 a.m. on 13 November.

I freshened up. By that time, Remya had woken up and made appams for me. I drank lots of water and had an appam. After that, I applied oil all over my body and wore my tri-suit. I had already packed all my things. My staff had also come earlier. They were excited. Venkat was with me. He was the one who had stood by me during my days of cancer and training for Ironman – from seeing me walking like a chimpanzee, to struggling with pain and finding it difficult to climb the stairs. He had seen me crying in the car for painkillers before my diagnosis. Now, almost two years later, he was watching me come back to life, filled with energy, gearing up to compete in the Ironman triathlon. A week ago, he had gone to Tirupati and donated his hair, praying for my success.

On the day of the event, Venkat had also asked my cycle technician, Mehboob, to check my cycle, tyres, chain and other parts. Mehboob confirmed that everything was fine. I had my spare tube, the tools to change the tube and an artificial oxygen pump, all in the pouch under my bike seat, which made it pretty heavy. I had six bottles of water, bananas, food gels and energy bars. I also had my shoes, eye gear, cap, helmet, gloves and towels.

I met Satish, the man who introduced me to the Ironman world. He was also participating. I placed my cycle on the bike rack and kept all my stuff underneath it, covering them with towels to avoid disturbance. I wore my swimming goggles, put some water in them, and wore them again to check if they were okay. The organizers had categorized the participants into three groups based on their swimming speed, which we had filled in during registration. These groups were green, white and orange. Green caps were the fastest swimmers. I chose white. Green-cap swimmers were allowed to go first, followed by white, then orange. Neil and Indrajeet had suggested I opt for the white group. I did my warm-up, a routine that had become automatic after nine months of practice, starting from the foot to the neck, covering all body parts.

To prevent fogging, I let some water into my goggles and then started walking towards the swimming area, praying all the while. I wanted to be an Ironman. Before heading to the swimming point, the organizers tied a band around my arm and wrote 0973 on it. I met Neil, my coach and guru, and took his blessings. I asked where Indrajeet was; he was a volunteer in the sea. It was a long walk, so I decided to return to my group of white caps. I looked for Gaurav, my swimming partner, and finally found him. He was also in the white cap group. All my swimming training partners were in the same group, trained by Indrajeet. Our running and cycling events were trained by Agnel, so we were all in the same-coloured suit. Aldia, Sidd, Agnel's wife Fathima, Dr Sujoy and Dr Keith were all there, my good friends. Everyone was excited.

The IGP was also participating. He had partnered up for a relay with Shobith IPS, then SP North, also my colleague. Shobith was doing the cycling part, and one of his friends was doing the running bit. We were all ready. By 7 a.m., everyone was behind the starting line. I was anxious but remained near Gaurav. I turned to him and said inaudibly, 'Come on Gaurav, make me qualify.'

The chief minister was going to flag off the race. He arrived. Because the cycling route was not yet ready, the event was getting delayed. It was supposed to start at 7 a.m., but it was already 7:30 a.m. Finally, everything was ready only by 7:40 a.m. To my surprise, the chief minister remembered I was participating and, along with the IGP, invited me onto the stage. We all faced the crowd and posed for pictures before the event began. To prevent the water in my swimming goggles from spilling out, I kept them on. After that, I immediately went back to my group.

Compared to the swimming course in which we trained, the Ironman course was very well-defined. There were big buoys at the main turns, and after every 50 metres, there were smaller orange buoys. We had to go into the sea, swim towards a big orange buoy that was six feet tall, take a left, and swim for a long time, parallel to the shore. At the next big orange buoy, we had to take a left turn, swim and exit. After the exit, we had to again get into the sea; this time, into a course closer to shore. There were yellow buoys to mark the return course. In the return course, all the turns were towards the right.

I switched my Garmin watch on and set it to open-water swimming. The race was flagged off with a loud cheer. The greens all went into the water. Now the whites stood at the ready. I stood in the line behind Gaurav, and we went to the starting point. Forty minutes of waiting for the flag off, that too standing, had made me a little tired. In fact, my knees, which had pain earlier, also started hurting. But this was not the time to think negatively. Focus on Ironman. Today is the day. Even if there is pain, finish the race. I had to push myself.

Next, it was my row's turn. We stood behind the stop gate, and after six seconds, when the row ahead of me left, the whistle blew, and the race started. As soon as I passed the starting area, I started the tracker on my watch. I ran slowly into the sea, keeping close to the line rope. I walked until the water was up to my neck, then launched into a swim with full energy. I kept looking for Gaurav, but he was faster; swimming during training and swimming at the event were not the same. At the event, more than 1,000 people were swimming to qualify. Most were going fast to improve their timing, while others aimed to complete the event in their best time. Everyone swam differently: some freestyle, some breaststroke, some butterfly and some without any distinct style.

In breaststroke, after every stroke, the legs move apart, kicking wide. In butterfly stroke, the hands move very wide and fast. Unlike swimming pools, there are no designated lanes in the sea. All swimmers want to stay close to the buoys and ropes to avoid drifting away. In a hurry, people bump into each other constantly. The problem is that if they kick or hit your goggles, there's a chance they might break or shift, allowing seawater to enter and cloud your vision. There's also the risk of injury; hands can get entangled, possibly causing shoulder injuries. I was hit twice. Swimmers were overtaking me, and for the first time I saw myself overtaking others as well.

After every five strokes, I'd look for Gaurav. I could see him initially, but not anymore. Everyone looked so similar; the only identifying feature was the cap they were wearing. I could see green caps behind me. I swam with full strength, taking a breath after every second stroke. In no time, I reached the first buoy and took a left turn. I got a kick to my face from a guy doing breaststroke ahead of me. Another lady hit me with her knee on my goggles. Thankfully, they didn't budge.

I couldn't see Gaurav, but I spotted Dr Sujoy swimming at nearly the same speed as me. If you don't fix a target for yourself or single out your competition, swimming can be very boring; the urge to overtake is what gives you speed. I tried to overtake Dr Sujoy, who is also a good swimmer. I reached the next buoy, where I had to take a left turn. After that, I couldn't spot Dr Sujoy anymore. From there, I swam fast towards the first exit on the beach. I wanted to walk as soon as I reached depths where my legs could touch the sea floor. I tried twice, but my feet couldn't reach. Another problem was the fast swimmers coming from the opposite side. I moved to the right, and after about fifty strokes, I was able to touch the sea floor. I saw Dr Sujoy right in front of me and then saw Gaurav re-entering for his return lap. I walked and then slowly ran. My staff, Venkat and Suraj, along with many other people, were cheering me on. I could hear, 'Sir, you're doing great, keep going!'

I wasn't tired, and I wanted to finish the swimming leg of the event. I checked the time; it had only been twenty-five minutes – I was well within time. But I didn't remove my goggles. I ran onto the time belt and back towards the sea. Again, I walked until the water was up to my neck and then started swimming. I swam without checking where I was going and ended up colliding with a swimmer coming from the opposite side. That's when I noticed I was on the wrong route; I had drifted too far to the left. I immediately started sighting. This time the path was marked by yellow buoys. I didn't have anyone to target, so I kept aiming for the buoys. After passing one yellow buoy, the next one became my target. There was a lot of space to swim as the swimmers were scattered. I noticed I was swimming with some green caps. I kept extending my hands and pushing forward. Finally, I reached the last yellow buoy, where I had to take a right. I took a right turn and kept swimming until I could touch my feet to the sea floor.

I started walking, and when I could run, I started running. Indrajit had trained us to exit as well. While exiting, I removed my goggles and cap and started running towards the cycling area. It was a long run. 600 metres. Before starting, as soon as I passed the time arc, I stopped the swimming workout on my watch. I wanted to see my timing. I could hear someone jokingly screaming at me, 'You are well within time.' I laughed and checked my timing anyway. I had qualified, and I had done it in my best time: 48.42 minutes at a speed of 2.34 minutes/100 metres. The biggest hurdle was over. I laughed and thanked God, smiling, and in that spirit, started jogging. I had time now. Conserving energy was more important. There were 90 kilometres of cycling left to do.

Running in the sand for this last stretch was tough. I felt angry at the Ironman organizers for not laying out a mat for the last 100 meters. The sand was loose, and my wet legs were sinking in it. Finally, I reached the shower area. I couldn't even control my pee. After a shower, I ran towards my stand. Drying my body with the towels, I put my goggles and swimming cap away, then had a big gulp of water with half of my energy bar.

I kept the gels and another energy bar in my pockets, put on my socks, shoes, helmet and gloves, and I was ready. I set my watch to cycling mode and checked the bike pouch – everything was there. One is supposed to take their bike onto the road before mounting it. Venkat was right there, taking pictures. As soon as I reached the road, I mounted my bike and rode on. Fourth gear in the front and fifth in the back. Until I got to Patto Bridge, I planned to keep them like that.

But like life, a bicycle ride can also be full of surprises. This time, it was not the tyre – the back pouch fell onto the road. I heard it and stopped cycling. What had happened? It turned out the holder had broken because of its weight. It fell right in front of an aid station. The young volunteers came running to me. One of them told the other, 'We are not supposed to help him,' but the other was ready to help anyway. I asked them with sad, beseeching eyes to aid me. They obliged and helped me tie the pouch back on. I couldn't leave it behind because it contained the replacement tyre tubes. I tied it back on but it was not a perfect knot. I lost five minutes in all this and now had one more thing to be careful about. I felt dejected.

'Focus, commitment, sheer will,' I reminded myself, and started cycling again. One year of training had given me a clear idea of how to complete the cycling leg of the event. The most important thing was to make sure your legs don't cramp. You should be left with enough strength in your legs for the running part that follows. Two hours for the first lap of the cycling track and two hours for the second. I had decided that my average speed would stay around 21–23 km/hr.

After Patto Bridge was the causeway; the most deceptive part of the route. I cycled at a moderate speed there. Suddenly, I saw Shobith cycling at very high speed and overtaking me. I was going at 25–26 km/h, and he was going at more than 30 km/hr. My competitive side wanted to overtake him. 'No, control! He is doing a relay. He doesn't have to run after cycling. He has another person to do the running for him. You have to run.' I controlled myself and continued cycling at my own speed.

Neil had advised me to keep sipping water every fifteen minutes. Two times during my workout, I had to stop because of poor hydration and a lack of energy. I kept checking the time to make sure I stayed hydrated. Every forty-five minutes, I was also supposed to eat an energy bar. Now I had completed the Bambolim climb successfully. Another problem that day was the sun. The race had started late and the sun was high up in the sky by this part of the event. The heat was intense. I sipped water every fifteen minutes and had a bite of the energy bar every forty-five minutes. The training had helped me drink and eat easily while cycling.

I reached the Zuari bridge. This was supposed to give me good acceleration, but there were strong cross winds blowing that day. They were so strong that they were actually lifting the bike off the ground. I could not ride fast enough, which put me at a disadvantage. The loss of speed had to be compensated for by pedalling. On Zuari Bridge, the effect of the sun was double as well. I managed to keep up a speed of 25 km/hr. Before Agaçaim New Bridge, there was a turn and just before that, were aid stations. I didn't stop at the aid station and went on ahead.

The return was the toughest part with the ascent onto Zuari Bridge. By then, the sun had started beating down hard. It felt like it was sucking out our energy. I didn't exert myself too much. Slowly, I pedalled through the climb and reached the church, the place where I had fallen that day, on my first ride along this route. After that, it was all downhill. Except for two ascents, the ride was relatively smooth. The pouch was holding up just fine. I made a turn at Dona Paula and reached Miramar. There were a lot of people waiting there to cheer me on. I checked my watch: 45 kilometres in less than two hours. 'I am doing good; one more loop and the cycling stretch will be over, too,' I told myself. But by this time, my bottles were out of water.

At the same aid station where my pouch had fallen off, I stopped and drank a lot of water. Tiredness had started creeping in. I rested for some time at the aid station, then resumed riding. The deceptive causeway made me very tired yet again. I went at a speed of 23 km/hr. After this was the Bambolim climb. Pedalling very slowly, I made the climb up. By this time, it was 11:30 a.m., and the sun was right above us. I was feeling like I was being drained of energy. 'Last climb, the Zuari, and it's over,' I reminded myself. I just had to reach there. But my legs had started getting tired by now. I switched the rear gears to low so that they didn't put more strain on my leg muscles. There was an aid station before the roundabout ahead of me. This time, I stopped to use the loo. I sat on a chair for some time. It was very, very hot. Even sweat had dried up. I stretched out my legs for some time and had a banana. 60 kilometres now. Just thirty more to go. I refilled my water bottles and started riding again.

Once I reached the bridge, I feel the sun burning my skin. I could feel it scorching my back. I counted each time I pedalled. And finally, I had made the climb onto the bridge and reached the church. My legs were still strong, though my tiredness was increasing. 'Don't cramp. Please, legs, don't cramp.' I kept telling myself, 'Keep riding at a speed of 22–23 km/hr.' After the Bambolim descent, I left it to gravity to cover the remaining distance. Almost at 75 kilometres now. 15

more kilometres to go. 'Come on. Just don't let your legs cramp.' At the Kadamba KTC Circle, I reached 80 kilometres. I was supposed to consume a gel now. My legs were slowly tightening up around my thighs. Setting the bike aside, I did some stretching. Cyclists passing me kept asking if everything was okay. I reassured them with 'All okay'. Slowly, I ate the gel.

I now had to reach the next aid station to get water. That was my next target. I again mounted my bike. My buttocks were hurting by now. 'Please, legs, don't cramp.' I rode at a speed of 21 km/hr and reached the aid station. There, I stopped again. Now there were only 7 more kilometres to go. 'Just keep riding.' As I reached Miramar, I reminded myself '5 more kilometres.' At Miramar, I could still hear a lot of people cheering for me. I saw Shobith cheering, 'Sir, great!' I felt happy. I took the turns before Dona Paula and I reached the end point of cycling back at Miramar. I got off my bike. My legs were tight, but not cramped. I took my bike and slowly walked to the designated spot. I kept my bicycle on its stand and stopped my watch.

It had been the longest ride. 88.33 kilometres covered in three hours, fifty-two minutes, at a speed of 22.9 km/hr. Forty-five minutes for swimming and three hours fifty-two minutes for cycling. A total of four hours thirty-seven minutes. Approximately four hours, forty-five minutes had passed. I now had three hours and forty-five minutes left to run the final 21 kilometres. 'I can do it. I *will* do it.'

I took a big gulp of water. I put on my running cap. I took my handkerchief in my hand, and started walking towards the running start line. As I exited the Miramar promenade, I started running. I was very, very happy. My legs had the strength I needed. They were not cramping. Only later would I find out that out of 1,400 participants, close to 600 hadn't even been able to complete the race because the majority of them got leg cramps after the cycling stretch got over. I started running cheerfully. During the run, I could hear Indrajeet's voice, 'Great going, Nidhin!' I saw him. I was very happy. He was standing on the side of the road, cheering me on. I ran close to him and told him, 'Just as you said, I completed the swim in forty-five minutes.' 'I told you!' he said and gave me a high five.

I ran, managing a pace of close to seven minutes for one km. The running route stretched from Miramar to Dona Paula; then a right turn and a run till the governor's house; a U-turn; and return to the starting point, where they would hand me a band. In this way, I had to complete three laps. Every loop, a new band would be given, which had to be worn around the hand. 7 kilometres, then another band at 14 kilometres, then another at 21 kilometres. The bands were in the colours of the Indian flag: saffron, white and green. During the first lap, I cheered for all the participants. I saw Gaurav returning from the first lap as I was starting. At the Dona Paula climb, I walked. After the climb, I ran. The first lap went off smoothly. I wore the first band. At every aid station, I stopped for electrolytes and water. I had oranges. After the first lap, the happiness started disappearing from my face. By 10 kilometres, they had vanished completely. It was midday. The sun was at its full height. My throat had dried up. '11 more kilometres and the glory I have been awaiting will be mine. Ironman. Just keep running!'

I kept aid stations as my targets, focusing only on getting from one to the next. There were three aid stations: one at the beginning, one just before the Dona Paula climb, and the last one at the turn near the governor's house. In a half marathon, the toughest part was between 14 kilometres and 18 kilometres. I decided I wouldn't stop until I had completed 18 kilometres. But I was drained by the time I got to 16 kilometres. After every 7 kilometres, I had a gel. From 16 to 18 kilometres, I had to do as I had done when I had first started training. Run and walk. I ran, I walked, and somehow, I managed to get past the last climb. Two bands on my arm now. One more band and it was done. 'Get that band,' I told myself. At the last turn near the governor's house, I stopped and took a gulp of water and electrolytes, and then started running.

It was very difficult to run. It was becoming next to impossible to keep going. I jogged then walked. The Dona Paula descent was difficult, too. My legs were starting to cramp. My vision was getting blurry. I reached the penultimate aid station. I had enough time left and only 2 kilometres to go. I drank as much water as possible. Neil had suggested trying out drinking a Red Bull before the final 2 kilometres. But because of the stop, I felt a little bit of energy. I could hear someone calling out to me from the sidelines. It was retired SP Mahesh Gaonkar, calling out from his balcony. I looked at him. I saw him, but I couldn't lift my hand. I couldn't even move my feet. My legs were cramping. I stopped and sat on the side. My body had given up. I tried to stand up, but my legs were like jelly. I could feel my thighs getting heavy like lead. I sat back down.

'What now?' Nine months of training. Before that, one year of pain and struggle. And here I was, so close to the end of something that I had wanted to achieve for a whole year. Something that was unachievable for Nidhin Valsan, if he had not been diagnosed with cancer. The cancer, the fight, the struggle and the pain made me realize who I truly was. That pain, that life in the darkness, in obscurity, in oblivion for one long year, they had built my spirit. That spirit had kept me going. A mere 2 kilometres couldn't stop me from reaching what I had trained so hard for. No one would have trained as meticulously as I had. I swam so much. I cycled so much. I ran so much. For what? For becoming an Ironman. Defeating cancer and becoming an Ironman within a year. To show the world that anything is possible, to be an inspiration, to be a beacon of hope for all the people fighting cancer. To remind them that pain is temporary and at the end of that pain lies happiness, everlasting happiness – it could be achieved, through patience, perseverance, hard work, focus, commitment and sheer will.

I was destined to be an Ironman. If not, then why would Ishaan and Niya be at the finishing line wearing T-shirts with bold letters, 'My papa is Ironman!' They were waiting for me. 'I have to reach them.' I had trained all these months for one photo with them in those T-shirts when I finish my Ironman, holding them in my arms and showing the whole world the pride and happiness in their eyes because their Papa was, in fact, an Ironman. Remya was waiting for me. She had to undergo more pain than me in this whole journey. 'I have to reach her.' The struggle, the tears – everything needed to end, there was happiness and smiles waiting for me on the other side of that finish line. My best friend Rony had flown all the way from Delhi along with Praveen (another good friend) just to witness my success. These 2 kilometres couldn't stop me now.

I stood up and I ran. With full strength and spirit, and towards my destiny. On the way, there were kids playing by the road, waving the national flag. I caught hold of my country's flag, and like an Olympic gold-medallist, I ran holding it high. Soon I saw the Ironman finish line in front of me. I ran faster. There were cheers and wild applause. I entered the final 50 metres where there was a red mat. I crossed the arch, and there I was.

An Ironman in 8:03:53 hours.

In just a year, I had transformed from being a cancer man to cancer survivor and, ultimately, an Ironman. Through unwavering focus, commitment, perseverance, discipline, hope, love, kindness, friendship, guidance and hard work, I defeated cancer and became Ironman.

# Epilogue

In July 2021, as I sat in the sterile silence of the doctor's office, a heavy cloud of uncertainty descended upon me. The PET scan, a beacon of hope after enduring six gruelling cycles of chemotherapy, had revealed a shadow of doubt lingering in my lungs. The doctors dissected my situation with a mix of medical jargon and grave concerns. It wasn't just a physical anomaly they spoke of; it was a spectre of fear, a possibility that my battle with cancer was far from over.

I was plunged into a labyrinth of medical procedures once again – a CT-guided laproscopic surgery was suggested to biopsy the suspicious area. But fate, with its ironic sense of humour, decided otherwise. The lesion was too small, elusive in its size yet enormous in the threat it posed. My doctors chose to wait, to watch, as I remained suspended in a state of agonizing limbo.

The next PET scan was scheduled for November, three months away. Three months might as well have been a lifetime. Each day was a page in a calendar, heavy with the weight of the unknown. The 'what ifs' haunted my thoughts, a relentless whisper that turned every moment into an eternity of waiting.

Stepping back into the familiar corridors of my workplace in Goa was like walking into both a refuge and a reminder of the life I once knew. My return to work, under the shadow of my health struggles, felt like a tentative step towards normalcy, a fragile bridge between my past and an uncertain future. My family, my unwavering support system, accompanied me, their presence a soothing balm to my tumultuous inner world.

My doctor's advice rang in my ears – to live a disciplined life, to nourish my body with good food and to shed the weight I had gained during my treatment. These were simple instructions, but they carried the weight of a much larger battle – the fight to reclaim my body and life from the clutches of illness. Exercise became a new addition to my routine, as I continued to be determined to heal.

I remember the call to my boss, the DGP, informing him of my return. It was a conversation filled with cautious optimism, tempered by the reality of my limitations. I could not manage fieldwork for some time. I was still healing, still vulnerable. My body, though on the mend, was not yet ready for the demands of fieldwork.

As I settled into the rhythm of my work in Goa, a relentless shadow followed me. The spectre of uncertainty regarding my health hovered persistently over my days and nights. Despite the semblance of normalcy at work, a torrent of negative thoughts began to consume me. They were like uninvited guests, creeping into my mind, poisoning my moments of solitude.

The thoughts were a chaotic mix of fear and despair. They spiralled around me, echoing the worst possibilities – what if the cancer had returned? What if I had to endure even more aggressive treatments? The prospect of more chemotherapy, of a bone marrow transplant, loomed over me like a grim future waiting to unfold.

The revelation hit me during one of those long, sleepless nights. I was a prisoner of my own thoughts, caught in a web of relentless negativity. It was Remya who first noticed the change in me. One night, she found me sitting alone on the sofa, with tears rolling down my cheeks. It was then that I confessed, 'I can't stop these thoughts. What should I do?'

Our conversation that night was a lifeline in the storm. Remya's words were gentle yet firm, her concern a guiding light. As I poured out my fears and anxieties, the realization dawned on me – I was depressed. It wasn't just the physical aftermath of chemotherapy or the social isolation that came with my illness; it was something deeper, a mental and emotional abyss that I had unknowingly slipped into.

The decision to seek professional help marked a turning point in my journey. It was a step taken with a mix of apprehension and hope, a leap of faith into the unknown realms of healing and self-discovery. My thoughts turned to Akshara Damle, an old friend.

Reaching out to Akshara, too, was a humbling experience. Once a mentor to him, I was now in need of his counsel. The irony of the situation wasn't lost on me, but it was overshadowed by a greater need – the need to heal, to find my way out of the dark maze of depression. He agreed to take me on as a client, offering to conduct our sessions online, a gesture that spoke of his willingness to support me in my time of need.

The therapy sessions with Akshara were like navigating through a dense fog that had settled over my mind. Each meeting was a step towards clarity, a journey of confronting and untangling the intricate web of my thoughts and emotions. Akshara's approach was both compassionate and insightful, guiding me through the murky waters of my psyche with a steady hand.

One of the techniques that resonated deeply with me was the 'magnificent Nidhin' method, as he referred to it! It involved visualizing a version of myself that was not shackled by depression, a version that was strong, capable and, above all, free from negative thoughts. This exercise was more than just a mental diversion; it became a glimpse into a potential future where I was in control of my thoughts and my life.

Another profound technique we explored was 'inner child healing'. This method took me on a journey back to my earliest memories, allowing me to confront and soothe the fears and hurts of my younger self. It was a powerful and sometimes painful process, but it brought a sense of closure and understanding to aspects of my psyche that had long been neglected and wounded.

Over the course of three months, these sessions became my sanctuary, a place where I could unravel the complexities of my thoughts and emotions without fear or judgement. Akshara's guidance was instrumental during this time, providing me with the tools and understanding to navigate my way through depression.

As the therapy progressed, I could feel the heavy veil of negativity lifting gradually. It wasn't an overnight transformation, but a slow and steady reclaiming of my mental space from the clutches of depression. The recurring patterns of negative thoughts began to lose their grip, replaced by a newfound sense of peace and control.

The culmination of this journey coincided with the start of my Ironman training. Soon the rigorous process also became a celebration of my regained strength, a powerful reminder of the journey I had undertaken to reclaim my life. The physical challenge symbolized so much more than just an athletic pursuit; it was a testament to my recovery, my resilience and my ability to overcome the toughest of challenges, both mentally and physically.

By February 2023, I had completed my manuscript, handwriting it day by day. Following my achievements in the Ironman triathlon, I also took on the role of SP in North Goa District, with the added duties of SP Crime for Goa. His Excellency, Governor Sreedharan Pillai, acknowledged my efforts, and the Honourable Chief Minister of Goa celebrated my success by tweeting a photo of me adorned with the Ironman medal. In October 2023, I once again completed the Ironman marathon, taking on the swimming and running segments solo, and joined by my partner from the Goa Police, Vishnu Gawas, for the cycling stage. Shortly thereafter, I was reassigned to the Delhi Police. I undertook a penance and visited the Sabarimala Ayyappa Swamy Temple along with my buddy Ravi Shankar Shukla, IAS, from Lal Bahadur Shastri National Academy of Administration in Mussoorie. As desired by Ayyappa Swamy, Ravi introduced me to Akshaya Bahibala, the author of *Bhang Journeys* and creative mind behind the indie bookshop Walking BookFairs. Thanks to him, I was introduced to Pan Macmillan India, and they agreed to publish my book.

However, as I finished reviewing the final manuscript with my editor, Isha Banerji, and prepared to send back the manuscript, I was confronted with daunting news. In January 2024, my cancer returned, evolving into an aggressive form of B-Cell Lymphoma. Currently, I am awaiting a date for a bone marrow transplant (BMT) – a procedure I had always dreaded. After enduring three rounds of salvage chemotherapy in March and April 2024, the upcoming BMT seems intimidating. Yet, having faced and surmounted numerous challenges before, I remain resolute. I never give up. *Ana la astaslam besahool*!

# Images

The QR code below will lead you to a page where I have documented through photographs my journey from being a cancer patient to training for the Ironman triathlon.